First published in 2023 by

 columba BOOKS

Block 3b, Bracken Business Park,
Bracken Road, Sandyford, Dublin 18, D18 K277
www.columbabooks.com

ISBN: 978-1-78218-396-9

Set in FreightDisp Pro 11/15 and Essonnes Display
Book and cover design by Alba Esteban | Alestura Design
Illustrations by Alba Esteban | Alestura Design
Printed with L&C, Poland

finding
HOPE

compiled by

SISTER STAN

* * *

This book is dedicated to Charlie Bird for his
inspiration, positivity, and courage in facing
and living with motor neurone disease.

* * *

TABLE OF CONTENTS

· ·

INTRODUCTION
. . . .

This book was set in motion in Spring 2022 when I wanted to do something to bring hope into people's lives. I was very conscious that we were living in extremely troubled times, with global poverty, climate changes and conflicts all across the world, such as the war in Ukraine, and the many manifestations of Covid-19 still affecting the lives of so many people. At the time I was reflecting on hope and the importance of hope in our lives. I was also reflecting on my own sources of hope, and I wondered how other people found hope.

I decided to compile a companion to my last book *Finding Peace*, which would explore the theme of hope and how it manifests for different people. I wrote to all the contributors to this book, asking them the same question: 'Where and how do you find hope in your daily life?' Even as I wrote the letters, I knew it wasn't an easy question. I was asking them to reveal what was a very private matter. But the response was wonderfully positive, generous and uplifting.

Practically all of them wrote back with an outpouring of honesty. The people I asked represented a very broad spectrum of Irish life. They included public figures as well as private citizens from every part of the community. Politicians, public servants, writers, artists, journalists, poets, priests, people in recovery, activists of all kinds, as well as private citizens, all responded in a most generous way, revealing themselves through *hope*. And their hope revealed myself to me, as I trust they will do for you as part of this ongoing process.

And so, the book was born. A great mixture of choice and memory. Every response was unique, every individual had something different to say, and therefore the material here is diverse and wide-ranging. I knew the responses were true and authentic. They were too personal, definite and quirky to be anything but honest, and this makes the reading pleasurable and engaging as we turn the pages from one person to another.

The higgledy-piggledy arrangement emphasises the richness and variety of the responses. The book offers serious and interesting insight into people's lives, and they all testify to an inner wisdom that is sustaining, especially in times of crisis such as now.

My intention is that you will find a deep source of *hope* in the book, as I did.

For me a short passage from Aeschylus helped me in my quest for hope:

He who learns must suffer.
And even in our sleep
pain that cannot forget
falls drop by drop upon the heart,
and in our own despair,
against our will,
comes wisdom to us by the awful grace of God.

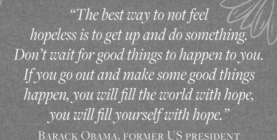

"The best way to not feel hopeless is to get up and do something. Don't wait for good things to happen to you. If you go out and make some good things happen, you will fill the world with hope, you will fill yourself with hope."

Barack Obama, former US president

* * *

"There is always hope for a tree: when felled, it can start its life again; its shoots continue to sprout. Its roots may have grown old in the earth, its stump rotting in the ground, but let it scent the water, and it buds, and puts out branches like a plant newly set."

Job 14:7-9

WHY IS THE NEWS ALWAYS BAD?

Bryan Dobson

The phone rang, loudly but not alarmingly, in the early morning darkness. The call was expected and the news welcome. Our daughter had given birth to a baby boy. Both were well. She was exhausted but exhilarated, the baby was sleeping. After she gave us the wonderful news direct from the maternity ward, we fell back asleep as newly minted grandparents.

New life gives new hope like no other human experience. With each passing month another landmark of infant development is recorded. First smile, tiny hands gripping your finger, first words, crawling, walking, and the slow but unmistakable emergence of an individual personality, a unique human being.

During close on forty years in journalism I have reported very often on failure and folly; at times on tragedy and anguish; and just occasionally on moments of great hope and soaring expectation.

Of course, none of those moments of hope can compare with the personal joy of becoming a parent or grandparent, and the intense experience that accompanies landmark moments in a life, but they do share at least one thing in common: a sense of starting anew and of endless possibility.

"Why is the news always bad?" I am often asked. "Well, not always," I reply. The page of history can also be turned to a new and more optimistic chapter.

Conflict, war, pandemic, recession, they all end eventually. And when they do, it is usually down to human skill and enterprise, and the belief of people in a better future.

Scientists give us the means to fight disease.

Engineers devise new technologies that transform our lives.

Entrepreneurs find new ways of distributing wealth and expanding prosperity.

Politicians deploy the skills of compromise to resolve disputes.

Artists reveal truth, helping us to understand the present and navigate the future.

My hope is in the child who one day will fulfil their own destiny and might just be that scientist, engineer, entrepreneur, politician or artist.

. . . .

Bryan Dobson is a RTÉ news presenter and grandfather.

"In the midst of winter, I found there was, within me, an invincible summer. And that makes me happy. For it says that no matter how hard the world pushes against me, within me, there's something stronger – something better, pushing right back."

ALBERT CAMUS, AUTHOR & PHILOSOPHER

*   *   *

"As it is, these remain: faith, hope and love, the three of them; and the greatest of them is love."

1 CORINTHIANS 13:13

RECONCILIATION

· · · · · · · · · · · · · · · · · · ·

Aaron Koay

I n all its incomprehensible complexity, the different colours, shades and tones, I have often thought that life is simply an endless cycle of construction and destruction of oneself. What an elegant yet despairing answer to the riddle of life that would be? So, I would run and run and run, just so I could catch a glimpse of that one true meaning of it all. Or if I could prove myself worthy, that life would show mercy and reveal its secret to me. Then, I thought, I would be hopeful.

I would be whole.

Yet, it would cheekily fleet, every time when I get so very close to it. And I would fall. And I would convince myself that I wasn't enough. I need to be better. Why am I good for nothing? I couldn't get out of my bed, yet I couldn't sleep. I am worn out. Why was I running again? I couldn't tell. I should see a doctor, I would tell myself, because I know I would do it all over again and again. Whatever it takes to make me feel alive.

But, maybe, it doesn't have to be like that.

There could, perhaps, be an alternative story to this passionate, masochistic and endless obsession of searching. Perhaps life doesn't demand an answer. Perhaps it is okay to feel like every part of me is at odds with everything and everyone else. Perhaps it is safe to admit that I am not – and will never be – enough, and that is okay. Perhaps there is a choice. Perhaps there could be a story of peace and hope where I am at my own mercy.

Perhaps life isn't that unkind after all.

Aaron Koay (he/him) is a migrant from Malaysia, a pharmacist, a researcher, an equality, diversity and inclusion activist, and an incoming PhD scholar in Public Health at University College London.

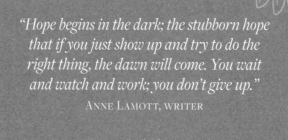

"Hope begins in the dark; the stubborn hope that if you just show up and try to do the right thing, the dawn will come. You wait and watch and work; you don't give up."

ANNE LAMOTT, WRITER

* * *

"The temporary, light burden of our hardships is earning us for ever an utterly incomparable, eternal weight of glory, since what we aim for is not visible but invisible. Visible things are transitory, but invisible things eternal."

2 CORINTHIANS 4:17-18

THE COMPASSION AND RESILIENCE OF PEOPLE GIVES ME HOPE

Mary Lou McDonald

People give me hope. People are amazing. Our young people in particular, with all of their talent, potential and compassion, fill me with optimism. This is a generation of young people that is passionate and enthusiastic about shaping a brighter future for everyone. I believe they will achieve great things despite the many daunting challenges we face.

They are calling out the fundamental inequalities in your society. They are calling out climate injustice. They are calling out deep social injustice. They live the values of community, inclusion and solidarity in a very open and honest way. It is a generation that is genuine about not leaving anyone behind.

Young people are holding a mirror up to our society and they force those of us who are older to see that reflection, warts and all. This demands that we ask ourselves some incredibly important questions about the type of world we want to live in. That is a revolutionary act in itself.

Young people are powerfully honest about how they see life; a pure certainty and clarity. They can really see the woods for the trees. It is such a great thing. I wish we could bottle it because I think it will help us to build a better, kinder, fairer world.

I love meeting young people. They bring an energy and a vibrancy that is really uplifting. After a meeting or a rally, they will often ask for selfies. I would stand there for hours to get those moments with those kids. Here's what I know for sure; what is given by way of respect, kindness and understanding to our young generation, our society will get back in spades.

For those of us in political life, our great task is not only to resolve problems in the here and now, but also to create platforms where the next generation can answer and resolve far bigger questions in their time. The optimism of this young generation to bring about positive change makes me hopeful, because I think that optimism is what has always driven human progress and societal change.

The resilience of people also gives me hope. Some people live extremely tough lives. They bear terrible hardship and suffering and yet they can endure, overcome and triumph. You see the human capacity for compassion in the trials of everyday life.

You see it in homes where there is serious illness or disability. In homes where there are addiction issues or violence and abuse. People can be confronted by incredible pain and they still come through it. I've always been amazed by that resilience.

The awfulness of the war in Ukraine would cause you to despair for humanity and for the fact that we are again living in a world in which the menace of nuclear weaponry is the bargaining chip between great powers, a world where tyranny can rain down violence and misery on people.

However, then you look at how courageous and resolute the Ukrainian people are. That shows you that humanity can endure and survive even the most horrendous situation. That has to give you hope. There is a natural human capacity to stand up, to fight back and endure no matter how bad or how terrifying things can be. I find that a very hopeful thing. It's a very moving part of the human experience.

Sometimes we underestimate people and we often underestimate ourselves. It is only when you see a very intense scenario like war, where people are brought to the brink, where they are tested to their very limits that you realise the depths of the human ability to overcome.

The dignity of human resilience is best captured by the phrase 'It is not those who inflict the most, but those who can endure the most who will prevail'. I think those words are a clarion call of hope for those who are downtrodden, experiencing injustice, and for those whose backs are to the wall. There is real strength in the belief that nothing is lost when hope persists.

* *

Mary Lou McDonald is Leader of Sinn Féin and Teachta Dála for the Dublin Central constituency. Mary Lou was educated in Trinity College Dublin, University of Limerick and Dublin City University where she studied English Literature, European Integration Studies and Human Resource Management. She is married to Martin and they have two children, Iseult and Gerard.

"The hope that is left after all your hopes are gone - that is pure hope, rooted in the heart."

BR DAVID STEINDL-RAST, AUTHOR & LECTURER

* * *

"Be strong, stand firm, have no fear, do not be afraid of them, for Yahweh your God is going with you; he will not fail you or desert you."

DEUTERONOMY 31:6

AN EXPRESSION OF HOPE

Abdulai Masaray

My name is Abdulai Masaray. I live in Dublin, and I am originally from Sierra Leone. I am an asylum seeker, refugee and migrant activist. I am allergic to injustice and want to help fight it.

In certain cases our hopes are not met, but more often our hopes are fulfilled unexpectedly and by people who we never considered or thought would help us; some hopes are even met by total strangers, or in a very strange way, by things or nature. Hope is that voice or feeling that inspires you and makes you forget, or sort of not too bothered about, your present circumstances.

I will try to summarise my own experience in pointing out my understanding of the word or expression 'hope'.

Early in 2021, I had a shocking and terrible experience, as I was kicked out of the Longford direct provision centre where I had lived for over two years. It was traumatic, as I had nowhere to go, and I wasn't provided with any sort of assistance from IPAS [International Protection Accommodation Services] and Covid was at its peak. Before that traumatic day, I had been trying to secure an apartment or a room, as I already received my residency, but it was not fruitful because most of the landlords were not willing to accept the Housing Assistance Payment (HAP). I was left in absolute limbo.

I decided to write a letter to the Department of Justice expressing my frustration about how I was treated and copied some organisations including Comhlámh - an association of development workers and volunteers in global solidarity, open to anyone interested in social justice, human rights and global development issues. I received a phone call from this wonderful woman called Niamh Phelan, who I refer to as my "God sent". She drove her car and picked me up in the evening hours and took me to her beautiful house. She then gave me a key to the house and gave me an amazing room. She said: "Abdulai don't worry, you are going to be fine ... please don't be in this house hungry, make sure you eat and please ... feel free to ask me if you need anything." Niamh gave me HOPE.

Abdulai Masaray is a mental health, human rights and good governance activist.

"Our lives depend on hope. If you have hope, you'll be able to overcome problems you face. But if you're without hope, your difficulties will increase. Hope is linked to compassion and loving kindness."

DALAI LAMA, TIBETAN SPIRITUAL LEADER

* * *

"Let us exult, too, in our hardships, understanding that hardship develops perseverance, and perseverance develops a tested character, something that gives us hope, and a hope which will not let us down, because the love of God has been poured into our hearts by the Holy Spirit which has been given to us."

ROMANS 5:3-5

REDISCOVERING HOPE

Adi Roche

M y husband Séan loves songs from musicals, and recently he shared a great song about heart and hope when I was recovering from Covid and feeling low and weary. A song called 'Heart' from the 1950s Broadway show *Damn Yankees*, where Coach Van Buren encourages his players, who have just lost again, not to give up ... he tells/sings to them that skills only get you so far ... but "You gotta have heart ... you gotta have hope ... don't sit around and mope ... when your luck is battin' zero ... mister/sister you can be a hero! You gotta have heart ... you gotta have hope!!"

Before I got Covid I had been struggling with the awfulness of the terrible war inflicted by President Putin on the Ukrainian people. In our charity, Chernobyl Children International, we were struggling to cope with the impact of the war, especially the plight of children in our care and the nightmarish invasion of the Chernobyl Exclusion Zone, the most radioactive/toxic site in the world as a result of the catastrophic nuclear accident in 1986. New releases of deadly radioactive contamination were produced by the Russian tanks, heavy artillery and even by trenches that they dug in the forests around Chernobyl. My thoughts were with the children, in families and in orphanages, those who were sick and/or disabled ... how could we help during a time of war and invasion? For many days we were despondent, overwhelmed, in sadness, despair and frustration at our inability to see a light, a hope that, despite the chaos and the fog of war, we would find a way to offer a helping hand and heart. Through long discussions, offering encouragement to each other, digging deep into our long experiences of strife and struggle, and ultimate breakthrough, we eventually found a path of hope; a way of help, hope and heart through the darkness of war. We brought food, medicine and clean water to our friends in the Chernobyl war zone, culminating in also being able to, through our sister partner Caritas, evacuate hundreds of children out of the zone and away to the Carpathian mountains, for sanctuary and restoration of their lost, stolen and broken childhoods; enabling the healing to begin and to give them a chance to have 'hope to hope' again.

We rediscovered our hope, we found our hearts ... and we rose once again and reached out with joy and resolve, and with the help, hope and heart of the people of Ireland we succeeded, both for ourselves and our dear children in Ukraine. For *hope* drives out all fear ... it binds us together ... *hope* conquers despair and restores our faith and confidence in ourselves ... and the power of the ordinary citizen to find the strength and vision to see a better world. "You gotta have a heart ... you gotta have hope!" For *hope* is indeed, the most enabling gift of all!

• •

Adi Roche is the founder and Voluntary CEO of Chernobyl Children International (CCI) and was one of the leading international figures to respond to the humanitarian crisis which ensued after the Chernobyl nuclear disaster in 1986. For over 40 years she has been passionately campaigning for, and is publicly active in, issues relating to the environment, peace and social justice.

"Hope is being able to see that there is light despite all of the darkness."

DESMOND TUTU, ANGLICAN BISHOP & THEOLOGIAN

✳ ✳ ✳

"Do not be afraid, for I am with you; do not be alarmed, for I am your God. I give you strength, truly I help you; truly I hold you firm with my saving right hand."

ISAIAH 41:10

SCIENCE AND PEOPLE BRING HOPE

. . . .

Luke O'Neill

Scientists have to be hopeful. They come up with an idea about something and then test that idea, usually in a laboratory. They are hopeful that their idea will pan out and that they will make an important discovery. It often doesn't work out and so they have to go back to the drawing board. One of my roles as the head of a laboratory in TCD is to tell people in my lab who are having a hard time to get back up on the horse. Perseverance, resilience, and perhaps most important of all, hope are what scientists and indeed all of us need.

That's what happened when the vaccines against Covid-19 were discovered, that liberated us. Scientists came up with ideas as to what might work. There was a chance that the vaccines wouldn't work or take much longer to develop. This is because Covid-19 was (and still is) a new disease and there are things we don't know. But thankfully the vaccines worked and have saved millions of lives, and will continue to do so.

I've met lots of people who are so grateful; such as older people who were stuck in their houses for months on end and who are now protected because of the wonder of science. I got sent a lovely piece of lace that had been stitched by a woman in her 80s. It had one word: HOPE. I also got sent lots of gifts thanking me for keeping the information coming throughout the pandemic and always reminding people: 'The Cavalry is coming.' I was so touched and encouraged by the kindness of people.

So when I'm asked what gives me hope, it is science. But not just science, of course, it's people too. The hard work and commitment of scientists everywhere. And the kindness of people towards their fellow human beings. This was so well illustrated by the huge numbers who took the vaccines, not just for themselves but for everyone else too.

We're at our best when we think of others ahead of ourselves. Deep down we all know that, and that's what brings me the most hope of all.

· ·

Luke O'Neill holds the Chair of Biochemistry in the School of Biochemistry and Immunology, Trinity College Dublin. He works on inflammatory diseases hoping to find new treatments for conditions such as Parkinson's disease, Alzheimer's disease and also Covid-19 which is an inflammatory disease of the lungs. In 2021 he was listed in the top one percent of immunologists in the world based on the impact of his research.

"If we decide something's hopeless or impossible, it will be. If we take action, who knows what we might manifest. Hope is curiosity writ large. A willingness to cultivate within yourself whatever kindles light, and to shine that light into the darkest places. Hope is the boldest act of imagination I know."

EDITH EGER, AUTHOR & HOLOCAUST SURVIVOR

* * *

"Have I not told you: Be strong and stand firm? Be fearless and undaunted, for go where you may, Yahweh your God is with you.'"

JOSHUA 1:9

HOPE ON A DIFFERENT SCALE

Nuska Yonkova

PERSONAL HOPE

I admit to thinking sometimes that I have no hope or that a situation is hopeless. Yet, I continue acting, struggling and living, which in itself is at odds with hopelessness. Hopelessness does not equate surrender; the same way hopefulness does not necessarily mean upbeatness. Hopeful, for me, means that you have to continue to do your best until you change the situation, all the while hoping for the better.

My work focuses on people who are the epitome of hope. They are victims of human trafficking. They retain hope in the darkest hours of exploitation, they keep their hope through the hardest of struggles to regain their self-esteem, and they rely on their hope to reinstall their existence within our hope-spoiled society. Sometimes, when I complain that I am losing hope, I should actually be ashamed. Because this is dishonest. The people I respect most have taught me so. I look for hope in their strength.

HOPE ON A GRANDER SCALE

The war against Ukraine, the atrocities, the impending danger to Bulgaria (my other 'home') and the culpability of the Russian people in all this weighs heavy on me and on my ability to be hopeful. To say that I

have been following the news since February 2022 is an understatement. I have been obsessing with all available news in the same or in an even more disturbing way compared to the 2010 'Troika' visit to Ireland or the USA elections in December 2020. It felt like losing hope, together with losing sleep and the will to go on. Initially. But then the Ukrainians proved me wrong. They did not lose hope in the face of a total lack of odds in their favour. They continued fighting and at times even prevailing, which changed the situation in a dramatic political way. This gives me the grand-scale hope.

Dr Nusha Yonkova leads the anti-trafficking work at the National Rapporteur on Human Trafficking (Irish Human Rights and Equality Commission). She had a similar role with the Immigrant Council of Ireland for a number of years before that. She holds a Master of Science in her native Bulgaria and a Masters of Arts from Dublin City University. Her Doctoral thesis at University College Dublin focuses on gender-specific assistance for sexually abused trafficked women.

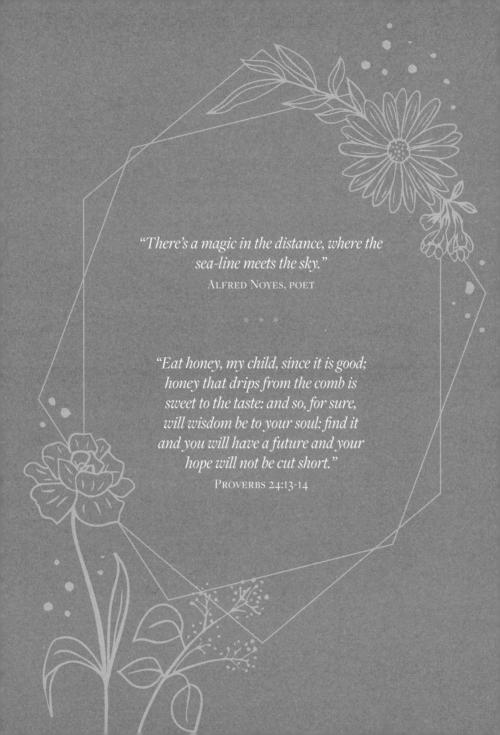

"There's a magic in the distance, where the
sea-line meets the sky."

ALFRED NOYES, POET

* * *

"Eat honey, my child, since it is good;
honey that drips from the comb is
sweet to the taste: and so, for sure,
will wisdom be to your soul: find it
and you will have a future and your
hope will not be cut short."

PROVERBS 24:13-14

GROWING HOPE

. . . .

Áine Lawlor

I'd hoped to have this written sooner. A mild kind of hope, but a humming in the back of my mind to live up to a commitment. A hope that I'd live up to my better self and actually write this piece. The kind of hope that plays a part in most of our interactions with other people, that we'll be better than our laziest or worst selves.

And hope keeps us going through the day; small hopes, but they hum away in our heads, keeping us going. That there won't be much traffic this morning, that the weather will be good for the big occasion, that your child will enjoy their birthday party. It's no big deal in truth if those hopes don't work out, but if they do, they're little victories in our day.

And a day without hope can be very long. Despair and grief are literally weighty; they bear down as soon as consciousness returns in the morning. They don't allow for hope, because the only hope, the return of a loved one, or a magic wand to resolve an illness or trauma, those reliefs are simply not there. What we hope for and yearn for, we can't have.

It's in those times I've found consolation in my garden. My love of gardening began in grief. The act of planting or weeding, focussing on one small patch of ground, paying attention to what your eyes see, and your ears hear, is nature's version of mindfulness. Or prayer.

The hope that comes with your seed packets in spring; promising a garden in your imagination that will defy the weather and the snails, and yield all that you have dreamed of in summer. The joy you share with other people who stop and admire the tulips or the roses. Or simply hoping the rain will stop. To garden is to practice hopefulness.

But there was another lesson to be found in my small garden. Even if the weather smiles on you and the snails avoid you, gorgeous summers will turn to misty autumns and cold winters. Nothing lasts forever, and time always takes its toll.

Normally, we'd associate winter with the dark and depressing times, and that's how I used to feel at that time of the year. But now the arrival of winter is the arrival of most hope in my season. It's the time when the pots are emptied and the garden cleared, and all the packets of bulbs arrive in the post.

Small, brown and unpromising, they contain a riot of colour - oranges and pinks, reds and russets, purples and peaches in the tulips, and yellows, blues and whites in the daffodils and early iris.

Some grey day in January, I'll walk in from work and notice a ping of white from the first snowdrops, signalling the colour explosion in store. Or there'll be a scent from a little shrub that hid its promise all year.

Those winter months, from putting the garden to bed in November and the first promise of spring in January, are now my most hopeful. Every time I look at the bare and dimly lit winter garden, I see those brown bulbs under the soil. They are the hope that carries me through those months, humming in my imagination, visible only to me.

Hope may be a small brown thing, under a blanket of soil in the dark times, but that hope, given a little nurture, brings me a rainbow of colour and great joy each spring.

. . . .

Áine Lawlor is a journalist and broadcaster with RTÉ.

"You need chaos in your soul to give birth to a dancing star."

Friedrich Nietzsche, philosopher

* * *

"So do not worry about tomorrow: tomorrow will take care of itself. Each day has enough trouble of its own."

Matthew 6:34

HOPE, WHEN HOPE SEEMS GONE

Archbishop Eamon Martin

When I think about 'hope', the verse on my ordination card comes to mind: "Be strong, let your heart take courage, all who hope in the Lord" (Psalm 31:24). I have been privileged during my years as a priest to witness hope in the lives of many people - even in the most difficult of circumstances. I can't imagine what it must be like to lose all hope. And yet, sadly we live in a world where too many people are in despair - sometimes turning to alcohol, drugs and other addictions in order to escape their fears and disappointments. Most disturbing of all is the tragic reality of suicide which steals away life and leaves behind a terrible, open wound.

A saintly woman once told me she learned the real meaning of hope when she was desperate and on the point of being overcome by fear and grief. She had more than her fair share of troubles - her husband walked away leaving her with two young children, one of whom died tragically in a road accident outside her home, and later she herself fell victim to cancer. To me her faith, and her hope, were palpable. She reminded me of the words of Jesus: "In the world you will have tribulation, but take courage for I have overcome the world" (John 16:33).

In the musical *Les Miserables*, Jean Valjean sings these words: "Who am I? My soul belongs to God, I know ... He gave me hope when hope was gone. He gave me strength to journey on."

To have hope when hope seems gone - that's the kind of hope I pray for. To know that no matter what the world can hurl at us, our Saviour Jesus, who died and rose again, continues to walk beside us, to show us the Way.

. . . .

Eamon Martin is Archbishop of Armagh and
Primate of All Ireland.

"*To love, means loving the unlovable. To forgive, means pardoning the unpardonable. Faith means believing the unbelievable. Hope means hoping when everything seems hopeless.*"

G.K. CHESTERSON, WRITER & THEOLOGIAN

* * *

"*All look to you in hope and you feed them with the food of the season.*"

PSALMS 145:15

A LESSON ON BEGINNING AGAIN

Brian Hayes

Since the onset of Covid I've increasingly become aware of many younger people who have either dropped out of college altogether or have changed from one course to another. We talk of the last few years and the impact that Covid has had on younger people, and yet I don't think we really understand the impact. I don't think we have any idea of the affect that forced isolation and social distancing has had, especially on people in their late teens/early twenties. And despite all the challenges of recent years - I think we are seeing some great lessons to be learnt for future generations. Lessons that might help us all to be able to admit when things are not going well - to admit that we all make mistakes. Rather than bottling things up, it takes great courage to admit that things are not working out.

And yet the decision to change your journey in life - even at a young age - is at one level an immensely brave decision. Continuing to do something that you don't want to do - either because of peer pressure or parental expectation - is not something that any of us should be proud about. I get great hope from those students who want something else - who are smart enough and honest enough to change tack and to admit freely that they selected the wrong course of study. I think that takes great courage. Rather than seeing this generation as an age group that are fixed on what to do, I think it's a very hopeful sign that people have the wisdom and capacity to say they want something else. That they are not going to be forced to do something that they don't want to do.

That is for me actually a sign of leadership, of maturity and hope. But it also points to a self-image that doesn't follow expectations. Too often people end up in careers and situations where they are extremely unhappy and dissatisfied. Standing up early on in life and deciding what you want, deciding that you may have picked a wrong course, deciding to rewrite your own life story, is something that we should recognise. They say the older you get the wiser you become. I'm not so sure about that. The Leaving Cert class of the last few years have come through a lot. I admire them and the wisdom they have shown in being able to manage change and being courageous in knowing when to say 'enough is enough'. Life is only ever a beginning. The capacity to begin again - is a marvellous attribute. A great sign of hope.

· ·

Brian Hayes is the CEO of the Banking & Payments
Federation of Ireland.

"Optimism is the faith that leads to achievement. Nothing can be done without hope and confidence."

HELEN KELLER, AUTHOR & DISABILITY RIGHTS ADVOCATE

* * *

"And all these things which were written so long ago were written so that we, learning perseverance and the encouragement which the scriptures give, should have hope."

ROMANS 15:4

THE MOTIVATION TO ENDURE AND

PERSEVERE

. . . .

Prof. Brian MacCraith

When one considers all the serious threats in the world today (war in Ukraine; Covid-19; climate change; global poverty), it is very easy and understandable to become pessimistic and demoralised. Hope is the counterbalance to all of this.

Hope provides the reason to persevere. Based on the belief that a desired outcome is achievable, however unlikely it may appear, hope provides us with the motivation to endure. Hope is a personal, motive force that provides us with the willpower to tackle challenges and the impetus to effect change.

In the words of Vaclav Havel, hope is "an orientation of the spirit, an orientation of the heart". Further, in distinguishing hope from simple optimism, he said that hope is "an ability to work for something because it is good, not just because it stands a chance to succeed".

In reflecting on my own experiences over the past twelve years, I had the privilege to both lead a wonderful university (DCU) over a decade that spanned the financial crash and the pandemic, and to chair the Task Force appointed by the Government to coordinate the national rollout of the Covid-19 vaccine. Unsurprisingly, there were many challenges and pressures in both roles. Throughout this period, hope was inspired in me from many sources: the boundless enthusiasm and positivity of young people, and the leadership shown by them in tackling the existential challenges of climate change; the resilience and generosity of Irish people; the innovation of creative minds as exemplified in the development of Covid vaccines in record time. One inspiring image is etched indelibly in my mind: the long queues of older adults, many relying on walking frames, snaking their way expectantly into vaccination centres in early spring 2021 – I then knew that the vaccination programme would work!

In conclusion, I cherish many quotations about hope but this, from Barack Obama, is my favourite: "Hope is that thing inside us that insists, despite all the evidence to the contrary, that something better awaits us if we have the courage to reach for it and to work for it and to fight for it."

* *

Prof. Brian MacCraith was President of Dublin City University (DCU) from July 2010 to July 2020. A physics professor, and a renowned researcher in the areas of sensors and photonics, Brian is a member of the Royal Irish Academy, and an Honorary Fellow of both the Institute of Physics and Engineers Ireland. In November 2020, Brian was appointed by the Government to chair the High-Level Task Force on Covid-19 vaccination and continued in this role until April 2022.

"*There is some good in this world, and it's worth fighting for.*"

J.R.R. TOLKIEN, AUTHOR

* * *

"*In hope, we already have salvation; in hope, not visibly present, or we should not be hoping -nobody goes on hoping for something which is already visible. But having this hope for what we cannot yet see, we are able to wait for it with persevering confidence.*"

ROMANS 8: 24-25

MOTHER EARTH

· · · · · · · · · · · · · · · · · · · ·

Cathy Kelly

Knowledge was always my answer to fear.
Know everything, learn everything, see everything.
This seemed to be the wisest way to know what was out there. To be present.

A fierce desire to help other people on our planet, meant I wanted to stand with and witness what other people suffered. In my work with UNICEF and in my previous life as a journalist, I felt that I owed it to the people suffering to try to understand what they were going through.

No matter how much it hurt inside, I had to keep my eyes open and watch the news to see how much work there was to be done. Famine, disease, hatred and war: how never-ending it seemed.

I realised one day that I was helping nobody this way. I switched off the news for a while and went outside.

I let our planet heal me. Give me hope.

I began to walk my three beautiful small dogs mindfully. Not the rushed 'must do this walk first and get home and write that' sort of walk. A walk where we examine the greenery and my beloved little girls sniff where other dogs have sniffed. In summer, they make little flattened paths amid the undergrowth, emerging delighted with sparkling eyes. In winter, they delightedly fling themselves into hidden paths, the muddier the better. We look at things that are supposed to be weeds and wonder why they became called weeds. I look up at trees that are part of an ancient hardwood forest.

I think that life continues in the same way these old trees have endured many years. The flowers pretending to be weeds, the trees and the loving eyes of my beloved companion animals; being with them gives me calm and hope.

* *

Cathy Kelly is the internationally best-selling author of twenty-two novels. She is a UNICEF Ireland ambassador and lives with her adult children and three dogs in Co. Wicklow.

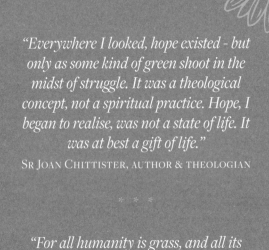

"Everywhere I looked, hope existed - but only as some kind of green shoot in the midst of struggle. It was a theological concept, not a spiritual practice. Hope, I began to realise, was not a state of life. It was at best a gift of life."

SR JOAN CHITTISTER, AUTHOR & THEOLOGIAN

* * *

"For all humanity is grass, and all its beauty like the wild flowers. As grass withers, the flower fades, but the Word of the Lord remains for ever."

1 PETER 1:24-25

'ABANDON ALL HOPE YE WHO ENTER HERE'

. . . .

David Norris

At the entrance of Hell there is supposed to be a sign stating 'Abandon All Hope Ye Who Enter Here'. This shows the great significance of hope in human life. In my case this is largely centred on my Christian religious belief, but I also take great hope from the song of blackbirds and thrushes, and the companionship in the garden of little robins. The stories of nature give one hope.

. . . .

*Senator David Norris is a former university
lecturer and a member of the Oireachtas,
serving in Seanad Éireann since 1987.*

"*Hope lies in dreams, in imagination,
and in the courage of those who dare
to make dreams into reality.*"

JONAS SALK, VIROLOGIST & CREATOR OF
THE POLIO VACCINE

* * *

"*I mean that the point of all our
toiling and battling is that we have
put our hope in the living God and
he is the Saviour of the whole human
race but particularly of all believers.*"

1 TIMOTHY 4:10

FRIENDSHIP
· · · · · · · · · · · · · · ·

Charlie Bird

What gives me hope now, even though I have a terminal illness, is very simple - friendship. Sometimes in this busy world we take things for granted. But when you are facing 'a dark moment' the kindness and love of other people helps to lift my spirits.

In the last almost six months I have received well over a thousand letters and cards from complete strangers from all over Ireland, and these amazing gestures have been so uplifting for me. I have made no secret of the fact that I am not a deeply religious person, but the hundreds of Mass cards that I have received, and yes rosary beads too, I accept in the spirit they have been sent to me.

Indeed, living through the last six months and the whole 'Climb with Charlie' event has made me realise there is so much love out there.

One of the side effects of my Motor Neurone Disease is that I cry every easily. Sometimes when I am out walking, a stranger will stop me and tell me how much they are thinking or praying for me. And yes, often times the tears flow. I sometimes bow my head to try and hide my emotions. But my tears are tears of joy and many times I show my thanks by hugging a complete stranger.

In my long career of over forty years in journalism in RTÉ, I have travelled the world and seen so much suffering, but those experiences are now helping me enormously, now that I am facing 'my own mountain to climb'.

On the 2nd April 2022, thousands and thousands of people climbed Croagh Patrick, as well as mountains and hills all over Ireland and abroad, in support of me and all the other people who have their own mountains to climb every day. The experience was so uplifting.

The hand of friendship is so important for all of us.

And I have learned from the kindness of strangers, that it is so important that we all extend the hand of friendship.

I have made one promise to myself now, while I am still on this earth, that I will continue to extend the hand of friendship to everyone. It might just be a simple gesture, but its effect can be far greater than you think. Just the simple action of shaking a hand or putting your arm around someone, can in many ways be lifesaving.

So please let's keep extending the hand of friendship.

· ·

Charlie Bird is a journalist and broadcaster.

"As long as we have hope, we have direction, the energy to move, and the map to move by. We have a hundred alternatives, a thousand paths and an infinity of dreams. Hopeful, we are halfway to where we want to go; hopeless, we are lost forever."

LAO TZU, PHILOSOPHER

* * *

"With a hope like this, we can speak with complete fearlessness."

2 CORINTHIANS 3:12

THE LUMP OF GOLD BENEATH

THE MANURE

. . . .

Choden

In these troubled times of environmental crisis, Covid pandemic and war in Europe, it is so easy to fall into despair and feel that humanity is doomed. In fact, my heart often sinks when I log into the news app on my mobile phone. This is even though I have been practising Buddhism for many years.

In times like this I recall a simple Buddhist story of hope. It is a story about a very poor person who lives on a heap of manure in a lowly shack. Throughout his life he bemoans his fate, and he passes his days in a state of both material and spiritual poverty. Yet, unbeknown to him there is a large piece of gold just beneath where he is sitting on the heap of manure. Tragically, he never comes to realise that all along he was richer than his wildest dreams, and worst of all, he goes to his grave having lived a life of poverty and never having discovered the treasure that was so close to hand.

In Buddhism the lump of gold symbolises our heart essence or intrinsic nature that is always whole, flawless and at peace despite all the ups and downs of our lives. It hides in plain sight in the simple awareness of our everyday mind. It is closer to us than our own skin, but most of us fail to recognise it. In Buddhist teachings it is described as our 'Buddha Nature'; although it could just as easily be described as our 'Christ Nature'.

The manure symbolises our issues, flaws and emotional afflictions. Just like manure, these seemingly negative attributes can be a source of spiritual growth if we relate to them with mindfulness and compassion.

At any moment, however, we can recognise the gold. What helps to bring the gold to light is to have compassion for the manure, both in our lives and in the lives of others. Then something can shine through, and our lives are subtly transformed. We touch something within ourselves – a still awake presence – that then informs everything we do and everyone we meet. Even in the face of life's greatest adversities we can rely on this still, awake presence and meet life's difficulties from this place.

In my experience this makes all the difference in the world, and it gives me hope. No matter how much suffering and confusion there is in the world, at any moment something can be touched and awakened in someone's individual experience, and they can learn to hold their suffering in a different way. It is like the lamp in their heart has been lit, and through their presence and activity they can then begin to light the unlit lamp in the hearts of others.

Choden is a Tibetan Buddhist monk who formerly practiced as a lawyer in South Africa and now teaches mindfulness and compassion widely in a secular context.

"For yesterday is but a dream
And tomorrow is only a vision;
And today well-lived, makes
Yesterday a dream of happiness
And every tomorrow a vision of hope."

KALIDASA, POET AND PLAYWRIGHT

* * *

"Then begins an existence more
radiant than noon, and the very
darkness will be bright as morning."

JOB 11:17

FINDING HOPE

· · · · · · · · · · · · · · · · · ·

Éanna Ní Lamhna

No one plants a tree without hope. In fact, no one plants anything without hope – the hope that it will take root and grow, produce flowers in due course and perhaps seeds or fruit later, depending on the kind of plant it is. Which is why being in a garden, working in the garden or indeed just sitting there relaxing, fills me with such hope.

It doesn't matter what season it is either. Even as early as February, the new green shoots of the spring bulbs poking up through the ground are affirmation that they have made it through the winter. The lovely crocuses and snowdrops will be visited by the early bumblebees on sunny March days, who will collect pollen and nectar from them to help them establish their colonies for the year. April brings the leafing of the trees – the tight buds unfold, and the leaves are a lovely light green colour. This is the month to start planting – even if it is only in a flowerpot on the windowsill, and watch the seeds germinate as the days lengthen.

I love summer in the garden – any garden really. The flower beds in the local parks or the wildflower meadows that are more and more a feature of public places, all are living testimony of the resilience of nature and its ability to spring back when these areas are managed in a lighter way. The bees, butterflies and ladybirds rejoice in these places, and so do I when I see the full potential that is there.

Nature responds gracefully to the passing of the months. Rich fruitfulness in August and September, glorious colour change in October and the elegance of the bare branches when the leaves have finally gone in November, all give me hope. And it's all still there sleeping during the winter months – just waiting for spring to come round again.

· ·

Éanna Ní Lamhna is an environmentalist, author and broadcaster. Her latest book, Our Wild World, *is published by O'Brien Press.*

*"All shall be well, and all shall be well,
and all manner of thing shall be well
... for there is a Force of love moving
through the universe that holds us fast
and will never let us go."*

JULIAN OF NORWICH, THEOLOGIAN & MYSTIC

* * *

*"Blessed are those who have not seen and
yet believe."*

JOHN 20:29

FIVE ANGELS GAVE ME THEIR WINGS

· ·

Chinonyerem (Chino) Okeke

H ope to me are the people in my life who came in at the time when I had given up or almost given up.

SARA GRIMSON

It was the evening that was meant to be my last night on earth. I had unsuccessfully tried to commit suicide the night before. But with the right Google search, I knew the right way to do it second time around. You called me a few hours before my planned action and gave me a lifeline.

SIS STAN AKA NAN

I was homeless and at the edge of giving up in life. I met you downstairs in the Immigrant Council of Ireland and you held my hand and told me everything was going to be okay. You handed me €80 that day which I spent on food and a hostel for a few days until I got the call that you had given me a home. This enabled me to study in order to access Trinity College. You were my hope.

PAULA MCGRATH AKA MOM

I came into your life as your cleaner and twelve years later I am your daughter. You were the first person that protected me. You showed me what it feels like to be protected. You gave me a home, you gave me a family, you gave me love and most importantly, for the first time in my life, I felt safe. You were my hope.

PROFESSOR BINCHY
I did not feel I belonged in Trinity College and I wrote a letter to drop out. You were my tutor and the moment I walked into your office, you gave me hope and stood by me for four years. You were my hope.

NURSE SIOBHAN
I had Covid and was all alone in the clinic the night my temperature was very high, and I was terrified that I was going to die. You gave me words of encouragement; soaked towels in cold water and soothed me with them. You were my hope during my biggest health scare.

So, to me, hope is the people that you meet that make a life-changing impact on your life.

• •

Chino Okeke is an Irish citizen, originally from Nigeria. She arrived to Ireland at 15. At the age of 17, after a trip to the A&E due to domestic violence, she was taken into State care. She became homeless when she turned 18; at the same time she enrolled in Trinity College to study law. She survived homelessness and graduated with a 2:1. She currently works in the Central Bank of Ireland and is also studying for her Masters in UCD.

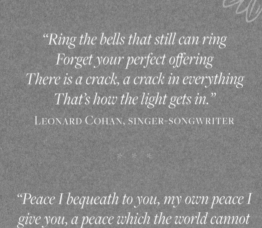

"Ring the bells that still can ring
Forget your perfect offering
There is a crack, a crack in everything
That's how the light gets in."

LEONARD COHAN, SINGER-SONGWRITER

* * *

"Peace I bequeath to you, my own peace I
give you, a peace which the world cannot
give, this is my gift to you. Do not let your
hearts be troubled or afraid."

JOHN 14:27

HOPE, STRENGTH AND COURAGE

Michelle O'Neill

H ope is what gives people the strength and courage to carry on with a sense of optimism and determination in their head that says things can and will get better.

As a political leader, it's my responsibility every single day to give people a message of hope; to take decisions, build bridges and give people optimism.

Hope is unity over division.

Hope is a better future for everyone.

Hope is a society where political leaders work together to make politics work and to transform people's lives.

That hope is achievable.

The scale of what has been achieved over the last twenty-four years since the signing of the Good Friday Agreement has resulted in the transformation of our society and communities, it has brought people together and helped realise peace on our island.

It has changed the lives of a generation.

And that didn't happen by accident. It happened because people had hope and worked together to show leadership.

They looked forward, not backwards.

If the two tough years of a global pandemic has taught us anything, it's that in the most difficult times imaginable, people need hope.

They need political leaders to deliver that hope.

Because it is the belief that even in the darkest of days, there is light at the end of the tunnel and the dark days won't last forever.

They will always pass, but you must have hope.

Let your hopes shape your future.

That is my commitment as First Minister Designate for All – not only to deliver a message of hope, but to make that hope a reality.

· ·

Michelle O'Neill, Sinn Féin Vice President, has been MLA for Mid Ulster since 2007 and served as Minister of Agriculture and then Minister of Health before being elected to the position of Joint First Minister. Following the most recent Assembly elections in May 2022, Michelle was returned as an MLA and First Minster Designate with Sinn Féin becoming the largest political party in the new Assembly.

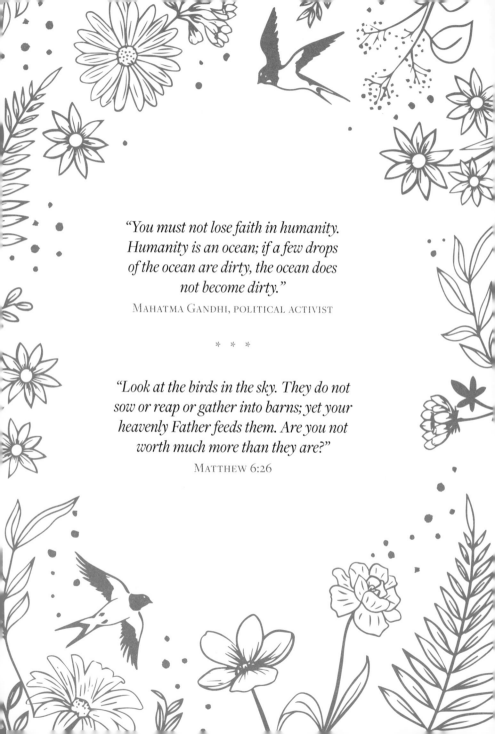

"You must not lose faith in humanity. Humanity is an ocean; if a few drops of the ocean are dirty, the ocean does not become dirty."

MAHATMA GANDHI, POLITICAL ACTIVIST

* * *

"Look at the birds in the sky. They do not sow or reap or gather into barns; yet your heavenly Father feeds them. Are you not worth much more than they are?"

MATTHEW 6:26

CIRCULAR ECONOMY OF HOPE

Colette O'Regan

When I was a young child growing up in Cork city, I remember the novelty of a packet of flower seeds popping through the letterbox each spring. A small simple paper envelope with 'Seeds of Hope' printed on it. I remember asking my mother if we needed to pay for them, knowing there was no money to spare, and she said "No, I don't know where they came from". For a few days we ignored the small packet, nobody else in the busy household even noticed it. Then at the weekend, I said to my mam that I was going to plant them. I did and totally forgot about them until a few months later some beautiful little primroses and marigolds appeared. What a gift from seemingly no one and nowhere.

Sources of hope in my daily life include nature - especially flowers - smiles and surviving suffering.

To everything there is a season, so it is said. When the season is dark, literally, metaphorically, one needs a source of light. As a closeted lesbian teenager in 1980s Ireland, when homosexuality was still criminalised, pathologised, and moreover a deeply shameful secret kept hidden from family and friends, I found hope in my own soul, which proclaimed "love is love" even if I dare not (yet) speak its name.

The Easter vigil ritual of passing the Paschal flame from one to the other, ordinary person to ordinary person, became the manifestation of my spirituality - we can provide hope to each other, we can light up each other's darkness, wherever we are. Living for long periods in West Africa and later in Southeast Asia my simple yet profound belief was firmly consolidated and constantly reinforced. Beautiful smiles lit up faces and hearts; hearts which had endured unimaginable pain and suffering.

'Chet laor' or 'a good heart' in the Khmer language is the most prized value in Cambodian culture. A good heart understands. A good heart forgives. A good heart finds a way to smile for another. I had the privilege to support oppressed and frightened LGBTQ+ people to discover their pride, discard their shame and revel in the rainbow. Smiles of connection. Smiles of liberation. Smiles of rainbow community.

Smiles - the lights guiding you through the oppressive darkness, into the technicolour of the rainbow and its hope and promise.

Back home in an older, wiser, more welcoming Ireland, I now work supporting rainbow refugees to find sanctuary and belonging here through Ireland's international protection and refugee protection programmes. A circular economy of hope. Smiles light up darkness and nurture hope. Let's be seeds of hope for each other.

· ·

Collette O'Regan works for LGBT Ireland, a national not-for-profit organisation supporting LGBTI+ people and their families through frontline support services, training and advocacy.

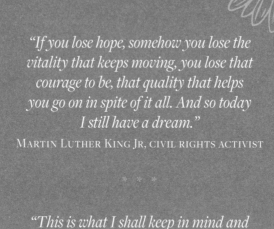

"If you lose hope, somehow you lose the vitality that keeps moving, you lose that courage to be, that quality that helps you go on in spite of it all. And so today I still have a dream."

MARTIN LUTHER KING JR, CIVIL RIGHTS ACTIVIST

* * *

"This is what I shall keep in mind and so regain some hope: Surely Yahweh's mercies are not over, his deeds of faithful love not exhausted; every morning they are renewed; great is his faithfulness!"

LAMENTATIONS 3:21-23

"WHEN ALL OF IT IS GONE...."

Colum McCann

Hope is the thing that exists beyond reality. Hope is that which remains, when all hope seems gone. Hope is brave enough to recognise the darkness. Hope knows that the world is hypocritical and cruel and ruthless, and yet it chooses to exist anyway. Hope is prepared to say that it is difficult to find hope, and to know that even this knowledge, in itself, is a form of hoping.

Hope is well aware of the sadness that occurs all around us, and within us, and through us, and by us, and beyond us; and yet hopes on.

Hope is not easy. Hope is not sentimental. Hope is not maudlin. Hope is not naïve.

Hope is muscular. Hope takes courage. Hope aches. Hope knows that it sometimes loses and yet it sticks around anyway. Hope is not afraid. Hope knows that despair is real enough to be dissolved.

Hope agrees with everything the pessimist has to say and then says, "So what?" Hope knows that the cynical tell the truth, but that it's a limited truth. Hope listens to the sceptic.

Hope does not dismiss the real. Hope enjoys difficulty. Hope goes against convention. Hope grows where hope was slaughtered. Hope is the wisdom that doesn't turn away. Hope enjoys doubt.

Hope plays the music contrapuntally. Hope is open to laughter. Hope is that thing which remains when the postman has been and gone. Hope is the orchestra in the bombed-out square. Hope is the roof over the houseless. Hope is the lone voice on the right side of history.

Hope comes from the ground up. Hope reaches across the aisle. Hope searches out the dark corners. Hope opens the curtains. Hope says that the impossible contains the possible. Hope exists beyond all available evidence. Hope is tiny and epic both.

Hope hopes for hope even when hope seems hopeless.

· ·

Colum McCann, born in Dublin, is the author of twelve books, including the international bestsellers Let the Great World Spin, TransAtlantic *and* Apeirogon. *He lives in New York and is the co-founder of the global non-profit story exchange organisation Narrative 4.*

"Dig inside. Inside is the fountain of good, and it will forever flow, if you will forever dig."

MARCUS AURELIUS, ROMAN EMPEROR & PHILOSOPHER

* * *

"There is always hope for a tree: when felled, it can start its life again; its shoots continue to sprout."

JOB 14:7

THIS LITTLE HOPE IN ME

Adunni Adams

When we wake up every day hopeful for something, this keeps us going, keeps us smiling sometimes. Hope is like a linking thread that connects us to life, it fuels us. And when we lose it, we find ourselves alone, in a state of constant dark sinking feeling, full of fear, no way out, no way forward, no way even backwards.

In my journey in Ireland I have found myself in such a heartbreaking situation, in the direct provision system. But I woke up, got up, had a shower, picked up my phone and searched for organisations that could help me out, and that is hope. While I got a lot of "sorry we are not allowed to get involved in this kind of situation" or "sorry this is out of our jurisdiction", I kept going.

I found strength in the little girl in me who had experienced so many horrors and somehow survived it all. That little fighter had seen death, she had been abused, she had known fear; she had feared for her life with every banging of the door in the dark hours. She had been alone in the room with an armed robber. She had bravely walked alone in the dark in one of the most dangerous places because she had to, even as she was terrified.

But look she had a best friend whom she looked forward to seeing every day. She loved reading historical romantic novels. She saved

up money to buy used books and she swapped with older people. She dreamed of a better future where she attained 'the highest qualification in education'.

Today, when things get tough I draw strength from little me who was born into a tough life but she somehow found hope. Over the years I have also been fortunate enough to have come in contact with some really beautiful people who make it easier to dream.

- -

Adunni Adams is a survivor of human trafficking crimes and a human rights activist. She is currently studying Social Policy and Sociology in UCD and hopes to build a career in social justice.

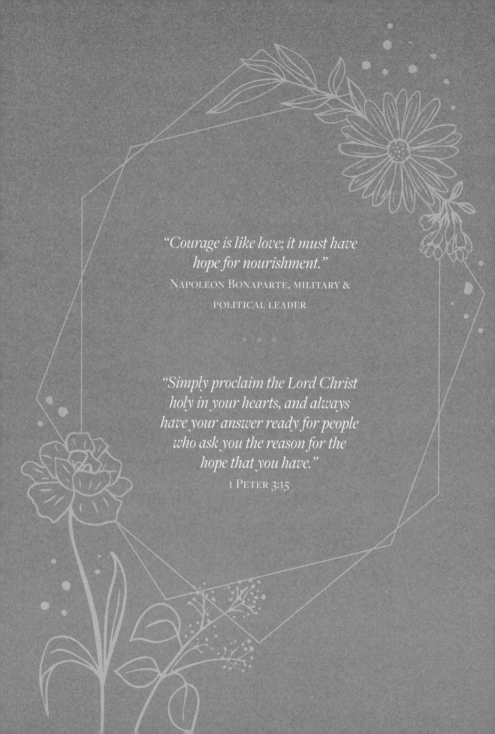

"Courage is like love; it must have hope for nourishment."

NAPOLEON BONAPARTE, MILITARY & POLITICAL LEADER

✳ ✳ ✳

"Simply proclaim the Lord Christ holy in your hearts, and always have your answer ready for people who ask you the reason for the hope that you have."

1 PETER 3:15

PURPOSE OF LIFE

· · · · · · · · · · · · · · · · · · · ·

Dalai Lama

I t's important to recognise that everyone has a right to happiness. There is no room for divisions into us and them. We need to think in terms of the oneness of humanity. Differences of nationality, race, religious faith or level of education are all secondary. We need to realise that other people's problems are our problems too.

Physical pain can be reduced through mental exertion, but mental unease is not relieved by physical comfort. We need to nurture a concern for others' well-being. Warm-heartedness reduces stress and brings calm to ourselves and to those around us; it gives rise to trust and trust leads to friendship. This I regard as a source of hope.

It seems to me that modern education by and large fails to foster inner values. Once children enter the education system, there's not much talk about human values. They become oriented towards material goals, while their natural good qualities lie dormant. Education should help us use our intelligence to good effect, which means applying reason. Then we can distinguish what's in our short- and long-term interest. Used properly, our intelligence can help us be realistic.

Many of the problems we face in the world today are of our own making. We are afflicted by anger, fear, jealousy and suspicion. Our modern education has little to offer in terms of achieving peace of mind. Although ways to tackle our destructive emotions are laid out in Buddhist texts, there is no reason why that knowledge can't be applied in an objective, non-religious way.

Such methods for tackling our destructive emotions are very relevant today. They don't involve temples, rituals, or prayers, but consist rather of a rational training in a secular context. Therefore, just as children learn the importance of observing physical hygiene, they also need to cultivate an emotional hygiene. This means learning to tackle destructive emotions and cultivate those that are positive, which in the end is what actually helps us achieve peace of mind.

With my encouragement, a new K-12 education programme has been developed by Emory University for international use. Social, Emotional, and Ethical Learning (SEE Learning), as it is called, entails a universal, non-sectarian and science-based approach to the ethical development of the whole child in the course of his or her education. SEE Learning provides educators with a comprehensive framework for nurturing social, emotional and ethical skills in their students.

If programmes such as this can be combined with modern education, they have the potential to be of great benefit. Results will not be seen immediately, but as a new generation is brought up to respect and implement compassion, I'm hopeful that more altruistic leaders will emerge.

* *

His Holiness is the 14th Dalai Lama, in a line of Buddhist
spiritual and political leaders of Tibet.

"Learn from yesterday, live for today, hope for tomorrow. The important thing is not to stop questioning."

ALBERT EINSTEIN, THEORETICAL PHYSICIST

* * *

"It was God's purpose to reveal to them how rich is the glory of this mystery among the gentiles; it is Christ among you, your hope of glory."

COLOSSIANS 1:27

HOPE — A FRAGILE PLANT

* *

Mary Harney

A life spent dealing with the ups and downs of the tide of politics, informs my musings on the condition of hope in the body politic. In my four years as Chancellor of the University of Limerick, I am greatly encouraged and can more clearly see the huge potential of our young people - talented, energetic and questioning - better prepared for their future than we were in the seventies! Cynicism is always present, but hope must prevail. Hope comes with courage, ambition and imagination; tempered by respect, charity and tolerance.

A lifetime in politics inevitably brings many seemingly intractable problems – 'the squaring of circles'. Solutions though are found with hope, optimism and honest communication, and not with cynicism, negativity and small-mindedness. Pragmatism and compromise are sometimes portrayed as 'dirty words' – but openness to compromise very often paves the way to progress and hope for the future. Obviously, not everything should be subject to compromise – politicians bear a heavy responsibility to the electorate as a whole. Responsibility relates to medium and long-term well-being, not solely from one election to another. Hope is long-term.

Hope needs nurturing in the turbulent world of today. Hopelessness and despair abound as we witness violent extremism and political trends barely concealing their underlying hatred of any opposition. Hopelessness and despair exist too in many wealthier nations, including our own. Hope lost takes time, resources, effort, determination and clear-headed policies to be restored.

Hope is akin to a fragile plant – it needs a reinforcing environment. In our connected world hope will thrive on a constant supply of honest, unbiased information – freedom of the press/media is vital but not at the expense of the promotion of hate. Promulgation of hatred along with wild conspiracy theories must be identified for what it is. Clearly, a tall order and an ongoing, difficult battle – nonetheless extremely important.

Hope's proponents must be courageous in speaking out - whether in politics or in everyday social interactions.

. . . .

Mary Harney is a former Irish politician who was Tánaiste and served as Minister for Enterprise Trade & Employment and as Minister for Health. She was the longest serving woman minister in government and was the first woman to lead a political party in Ireland. Having retired from politics in 2011 she now engages in business consultancy and is a company director. Mary was appointed Chancellor of the University of Limerick in 2018.

*"Set me adrift in a sea of hope,
And I'll set my sail to a new
horizon."*

AUTHOR UNKNOWN

* * *

*"This is the anchor our souls have,
reaching right through inside the
curtain."*

HEBREWS 6:19

PEOPLE POWER

. . . .

Dee Forbes

"Unlike cynicism, hopefulness is hard-earned, makes demands
upon us, and can often feel like the most indefensible and lonely
place on Earth. Hopefulness is not a neutral position either. It
is adversarial. It is the warrior emotion that can lay waste to
cynicism. Each redemptive or loving act, as small as you like
... keeps the devil down in the hole. It says the world and its
inhabitants have value and are worth defending. It says the world
is worth believing in. In time, we come to find that it is so."

NICK CAVE

For me, this captures beautifully both the power and the essence of
hope. No matter how bleak the circumstances, or how enormous
the challenge, it is the quiet but courageous belief that something
can be better than it currently seems, that can be the genesis of significant
and positive change.

Sometimes fragile, and always precious, it is often the quality which
ultimately finds a way to redefine frontiers and possibilities.

Over the past few years, as Director General of RTÉ, I have had the
chance to witness first-hand just how extraordinarily compassionate and
kind people can be.

The incredible generosity of the *Late Late Show* viewers across so many different causes was a privilege to witness. The solidarity, determination, and comradery I experienced on the recent 'Climb with Charlie' will live long in my memory.

What united these moments was a sense of shared hope, that by believing and working together, we can make a difference, and we did.

Hopeful people are essential in navigating life; and I am grateful for every spark of hope I have experienced along the way.

. . . .

Dee Forbes is the first woman to hold the role of Director General at RTÉ. A native of West Cork, Dee moved to the UK in 1989, beginning her career at advertising agency Young and Rubicam. She was President and Managing Director of Discovery Networks Northern Europe, before returning to Ireland to take up one of the most senior positions in Irish media.

"If you want to build a ship, don't herd
people together to collect wood and
don't assign them tasks and work, but
rather teach them to long for the endless
immensity of the sea."

Antoine De Saint-Exupery, writer &
pioneering aviator

* * *

"Rest in God alone, my soul! He is the
source of my hope.
He alone is my rock, my safety, my
stronghold, so that I stand unwavering."

Psalm 62:5-6

REASONS FOR HOPE IN UNCERTAIN

TIMES

· · · · · · · ·

Ronan Glynn

W e are living in a time of great uncertainty: the pandemic, a war in Europe, a global climate crisis, a domestic housing crisis, a seemingly intractable problem with access to healthcare services. And yet we can have hope that we can address these issues and emerge stronger from them. Why? Because we have done it before.

All parts of society were impacted by the pandemic. Families, communities and organisations were tested and stretched in ways which would have previously been considered unimaginable, with profound impacts on lives and livelihoods. And yet, through all of this, there were beacons of light; the remarkable response of those working across our health and public services as they met the challenges they faced with dedication and resilience; the rapid innovation, development and implementation of new ideas across all sectors; the commitment to examine and be guided by evidence in public policy making; and, perhaps more than anything else, the solidarity shown by people coming together in countless different ways to help one another; to solve problems collectively, to keep one another safe, echoing the meitheal spirit which has characterised Irish communities down through the generations.

None of this was easy. Certainly, none of it will be straightforward to replicate. We must ground our hope for the future in realism. And yet, we can be ambitious about what we can achieve. Indeed, we must be ambitious for the sake of our children and future generations. But we should be confident in embracing that ambition. Because we showed, as a people, that despite the uncertainty and challenges wrought by the pandemic, when we identify what is most important to us and when we focus on achieving those priorities, we can see old problems through new eyes; we can imagine something better, we can innovate, change and achieve something better, together.

Dr Ronan Glynn is a Fellow of the Faculty of Public Health Medicine at the Royal College of Physicians of Ireland. Ronan worked as Deputy Chief Medical Officer at the Department of Health from 2018-2022, was a member of the National Public Health Emergency Team tasked with leading the response to Covid-19 and was Acting Chief Medical Officer for six months of the pandemic. He took up a new position with EY Ireland as Health Sector Lead in September 2022.

"No matter how hard the past is, you can always begin again."

BUDDHA, ASCETIC & SPIRITUAL TEACHER

* * *

"You will have to suffer only for a little while: the God of all grace who called you to eternal glory in Christ will restore you, he will confirm, strengthen and support you."

1 PETER 5:10

REKINDLING SPARKS OF HOPE

Bishop Eamonn Walsh

Our lens on life will determine what gives us hope. Either life has a purpose or not; More later.

Convinced he was a dunce, on his fourteenth birthday Brendan, with his engraved smile, said goodbye to school and hello to cleaning the stables at a local stud farm. Amidst the mire and straw his smile reached the heart of the highly strung thoroughbreds calming their spirits. The natural horse-whisperer soon was to accompany the most famous at the Breeders Cup, Ascot, Longchamp and Kentucky. Using his natural gifts for a living ensured the smile never wore thin. Fulfilled doing what he loved.

Imelda, eldest of eleven, was bright but seldom attended school. "Has to dress and mind the others, himself is too fond of the sup," the mother confided in the teacher, who encouraged her to send Imelda to school even if late. Imelda attended twice, three times but rarely five days a week. She caught up quickly, leaving school at fourteen. Forty years later I met Imelda at her daughter's Confirmation; we chatted about school, the encouragement of her teacher, my mother. Later the principal told me Imelda was chairperson of the School Board of Management and of the Parents Committee. Every teacher has a similar story. Encouragement is the mother of hope.

Etty Hillesum, although destined for Auschwitz, insisted life is beautiful; keeping bitterness and hatred at bay through breathing life into the stagnant spirits of those who shared her fate. In the dark room Etty could see "the piece of sky" beyond her window.

Mandy, a chronic addict pleaded with the woman "give me your bag, I promised the priest I would not use violence". "She wouldn't let go but afterwards I phoned for an ambulance. Am I getting better father," she asked hoping for re-assurance. Hope is being willing to take the next step forward.

How we see the purpose of life determines where we focus our hope. For some it is everyone for her/himself; others see life as using talents to improve this world, handing it on in a better and more civilized condition than inherited. The lens on life will determine which tree our colours are pinned on.

Albert Camus saw life as meaningless; his life ended on a straight road where he drove into a tree. Was it accident or choice? Jesus Christ allowed himself be pinned to a different tree, insisting on showing we are one family; each uniquely gifted, entrusted to be co-creators and shapers of this universe, before we return to God. Seeing life through that lens helps encourage the giftedness of everyone while urging all to play their part with the hand dealt by life. Our default position is to cling onto life, like plants growing towards the light. For me life after death is a natural follow through to the source of all Life and Love, God.

. . . .

Eamonn Walsh, Emeritus Auxiliary Bishop of Dublin, is currently assistant priest to the grouping of parishes of St Mark's in Tallaght and Chaplain at Blackrock Clinic, and a former Prison Chaplain.

"It's always something, to know you've done the most you could. But, don't leave off hoping, or it's of no use doing anything. Hope, hope to the last."

CHARLES DICKENS, WRITER & SOCIAL CRITIC

* * *

"Those who hope in Yahweh will regain their strength, they will sprout wings like eagles, though they run they will not grow weary, though they walk they will never tire."

ISAIAH 40:31

WORDS FOR LIFE

· · · · · · · · · · · · · · · · · · · ·

Eileen Dunne

As a young girl, I went to Manor House School, Raheny, which was run by an order of nuns called the Poor Servants of the Mother of God. It was the early 1970s, 'women's lib' was just evolving, but those nuns sent us out into the world to be the best that we could be! Around that time, *Desiderata*, a poem set to music, became a big hit and most of us had the poster up on our bedroom walls. For our Graduation Mass in 1975, the nuns included the words of the poem in the missalette. I thought it was an inspired move and I have it still. I must also say that the older I get the more the words resonate with me ... giving me a good template for living the best and most hopeful life I can ... its provenance has been debated over the years but it's now widely credited to Max Ehrmann. I reproduce it here:

DESIDERATA – WORDS FOR LIFE
Go placidly amid the noise and haste,
and remember what peace there may be in silence.
As far as possible and without surrender
be on good terms with all persons.

Speak your truth quietly and clearly;
and listen to others,
even the dull and ignorant;
they too have their story.

Avoid loud and aggressive persons,
they are vexations to the spirit.
If you compare yourself with others,
you may become vain and bitter;
for always there will be greater and lesser persons than yourself.
Enjoy your achievements as well as your plans.

Keep interested in your own career, however humble;
it is a real possession in the changing fortunes of time.
Exercise caution in your business affairs;
for the world is full of trickery.
But let this not blind you to what virtue there is;
many persons strive for high ideals;
and everywhere life is full of heroism.

Be yourself.
Especially, do not feign affection.
Neither be cynical about love;
for in the face of all aridity and disenchantment
it is as perennial as the grass.

Take kindly the counsel of the years,
gracefully surrendering the things of youth.

Nurture strength of spirit to shield you in sudden misfortune.
But do not distress yourself with wild imaginings.
Many fears are born of fatigue and loneliness.
Beyond a wholesome discipline,
be gentle with yourself.

You are a child of the universe,
No less than the trees and the stars;
you have a right to be here.
And whether or not it is clear to you,
No doubt the universe is unfolding as it should.

Therefore be at peace with God,
Whatever you conceive him to be,
And whatever your labours and aspirations,
In the noisy confusion of life keep peace with your soul.

With all its sham, drudgery and broken dreams,
it is still a beautiful world.
Be cheerful.
Strive to be happy.

· ·

*Eileen Dunne is a senior Newscaster with RTÉ. A native of
Dublin, she is married to the actor Macdara Ó Fátharta and
they have one son, Cormac.*

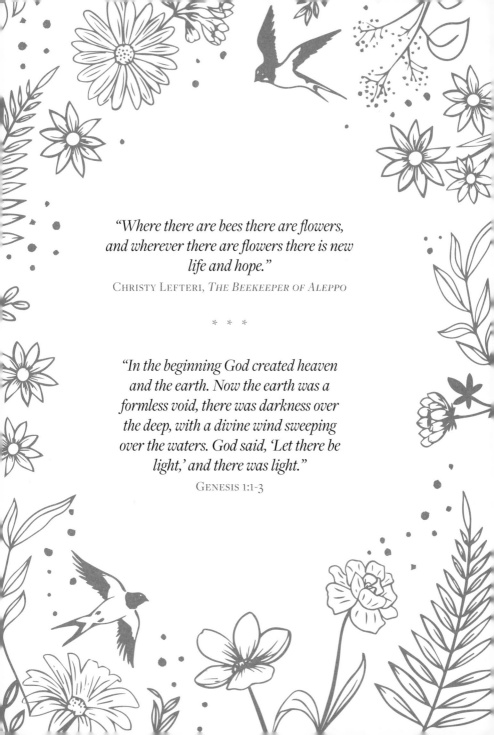

"Where there are bees there are flowers, and wherever there are flowers there is new life and hope."

CHRISTY LEFTERI, *THE BEEKEEPER OF ALEPPO*

* * *

"In the beginning God created heaven and the earth. Now the earth was a formless void, there was darkness over the deep, with a divine wind sweeping over the waters. God said, 'Let there be light,' and there was light."

GENESIS 1:1-3

THROWING OURSELVES INTO HOPE

Fintan O'Toole

Hope, as the philosopher Ernest Bloch put it, is an emotion that requires people to "throw themselves actively into what is becoming". It's not a passive feeling – it's one we choose. We open ourselves to what is "becoming", which I take to mean the pulse of possibility that we can feel all around us. Dread and darkness and despair are around us too, of course – and sometimes in us. But we live in a world that is always creating itself and we can make the choice to belong to that process of creation.

I find hope in the everyday evidence that most people, unless their instincts are distorted by whipped-up fear and manufactured hatred, are compassionate, decent and benign. I find it in time spent with children – the wonder of language, the endless curiosity, the energy of a world being explored as if for the first time. I find it in art, which can take us all back into that same state of wonder at the human ability to transform even the bleakest of experiences into beauty. I find it in the cycle of the seasons, nature's ability, given half a chance, to regenerate itself and, in doing so, to regenerate us.

So I think of hope as something that's already out there in the world. Throwing ourselves into hope is like plunging into the sea. It can be a bit of a shock, and the wind and waves are often against us. But it wakes us up. It brings us alive and connects us to things that are bigger than ourselves.

Things can and do get better. People can live richer, freer, more fulfilling lives. We have the collective capacities to live on the earth without destroying it or each other. There is hope for us yet.

. . . .

Fintan O'Toole is a columnist with the Irish Times *and the author of a number of books, most recently* We Don't Know Ourselves: A Personal History of Ireland Since 1958.

"All the darkness in the world cannot extinguish the light of a single candle."

ST FRANCIS OF ASSISI, FRIAR & MYSTIC

* * *

"Let us keep firm in the hope we profess, because the one who made the promise is trustworthy."

HEBREWS 10:23

THE GIFT OF HOPE

. . . .

Gerard McCarthy

Lisel Mueller wrote that hope "is the singular gift we cannot destroy in ourselves".

It has taken me years to realise that hope is a gift given by God to help us along life's journey. Hope, if I cooperate with it, will always open my eyes to something bigger than myself.

In Mark 4:26-29, Jesus tells one of his shortest parables: "He said, 'The kingdom of God is as if someone would scatter seed on the ground, and would sleep and rise night and day, and the seed would sprout and grow, he does not know how. The earth produces of itself, first the stalk, then the head, then the full grain in the head. But when the grain is ripe, at once he goes in with his sickle, because the harvest has come.'" (Mk 4:26-29)

The sower sows, trusting, hoping that growth will happen. His or her job is to put the seed in contact with the soil, but the same sower has no control over the growth itself. I still strive as if everything depends on me, but I know now that everything depends on God. My work, my contribution, is necessary, but it doesn't define the outcome. This parable of the seed has helped me over the years to slow down; to see the bigger picture, to renounce control and see life in its proper perspective.

Hope is the firm belief that when I play my part, God also acts. So I can live my life without anxiety. I 'plant and water,' but it is God who makes things grow! Despite setbacks, negativity, and failure, hope assures me that God's bigger plan is unfolding and the outcome is secure. God's promises will always be fulfilled: there will be a harvest and it will be good.

Gerard McCarthy is a priest of the Divine Word Missionaries and is presently working in the Diocese of Galway.

"I hope you find joy in the great things of life – but also in the little things. A flower, a song, a butterfly on your hand."

ELLEN LEVINE, AUTHOR

* * *

"Confident because there is hope; after your troubles, you will sleep secure."

JOB 11:18

A HARD ROAD LIGHTENED BY LOVE AND
THE GOODNESS OF PEOPLE

Gladys Lydon

A sense of deep foreboding was present for both of us as we drove from our home in Co. Kilkenny to Beaumont hospital in Dublin. My husband Patrick was having increasing weakness in his back and legs for the past six months and all medical investigations had drawn a blank. Now we were on our way to a world specialist in Motor Neuron Disease (MND), Dr Orla Hardiman. I refused to think that diagnosis belonged to Patrick, holding onto hope to the last. Patrick was convinced otherwise. As soon as the words Motor Neuron were mentioned he knew.

It was sobering to be in the waiting room with people of different manifestations of disability. I inwardly clung to hope that whatever was going on with Patrick, he will get better. He was such a strong, fit, vibrant man; forever planning inspired social projects that would benefit people disadvantaged by different challenges.

There was little medical investigation needed when we finally met Dr Hardiman. Out of her vast experience she confirmed Patrick had MND. We knew enough about the illness to know the prognosis; life expectancy typically was two years, more or less.

In that moment our world as we knew it changed ...

Patrick lived only ten months after that fateful day.

These ten months, however, were filled with love, warmth, friendship and hope. I lived with the words of Julian of Norwich "All shall be well, and all shall be well, and all manner of thing shall be well".

The ten months were blessed.

For the forty-four years of our marriage, we had lived in Camphill; intentional communities with people with support needs. It was humanly rich and rewarding, more so because we had, amid the community, our own family of four wonderful children. Now through Patrick's illness we too had support needs, and our community came to our home surrounding us with help and friendship of all kinds; from cooking us meals, to raising money for a wheelchair car, to building an extension to our house to accommodate Patrick's rapidly deteriorating mobility. Family, friends, and professionals made it possible for Patrick to be cared for at home. Over the sun-filled summer a constant stream of friends from different times in our lives came to have their last conversations with Patrick.

Five months have passed since Patrick left this earthly world.

Reflecting now on hope it is the goodness of people, the love we as a couple and as a family felt for each other, the belief in the Spirit, that everything happens for a reason, that gave me hope which lightened up an otherwise heartrending journey, every step of the way.

. . . .

Gladys Lydon, originally from Scotland, has lived and worked in Camphill Communities for the past 50 years, most of them in Ireland. A mother, teacher, homemaker and social therapist, she shared life with children and adults with support needs as well as with countless wonderful volunteers from all over the world. Living the dream she and her husband had shared, she is now growing flowering plants in a beautiful walled garden as part of a socially inclusive project in Westcourt, Callan, Co. Kilkenny.

"To live without hope is to cease to live."

Fyodor Dostoyevsky, writer

* * *

"Only faith can guarantee the blessings that we hope for, or prove the existence of realities that are unseen."

Hebrews 11:1

REASONS TO BE CHEERFUL

Ivana Bacik

Sometimes everything can seem hopeless. The aftermath of the Covid-19 pandemic, the brutal Russian war upon Ukraine, the existential threat of climate change, the ominous rise in the cost of living. And closer to home, the tragic death through suicide of a dear friend. All these factors and more contributed to an erosion of hope for me at a particular time. As a result, I found it difficult for my natural optimism (which I had always taken for granted) to re-assert itself.

What helped? Along with the great support of family and friends, I discovered two vital hope restoration methods; a strict ritual of talking to myself (not out loud!) every day - and an immersion in the sea at least once a week.

Each morning, I would remind myself about how important it is to identify as a natural optimist, even when not feeling a bit like being one; I would remember the great Ian Dury line that there are 'reasons to be cheerful', and that there would be things to look forward to every day – starting with the first cup of morning coffee. It may sound cheesy, but that daily ritual really helped.

The outings to the coast were even more important. During lockdowns, a few of us had discovered the blissful escape and immense physical/mental benefit involved in having a sea swim together at least

once a week; and our saltwater excursions have continued ever since. Nothing beats the incredible restorative joy experienced in stepping off the ladder at the Half Moon club on the wonderful old South Wall pier in Dublin. Basking in the clear cold water in sunshine, rain or even sleet, floating with toes in the air under the iconic gaze of the Poolbeg Chimneys – that's when I feel most human, most happy and most hopeful.

Ivana Bacik is Labour TD for Dublin Bay South (elected July 2021), a barrister and Leader of the Labour Party since March 2022. She previously served as a Dublin University Senator (first elected 2007; re-elected 2011, 2016 and 2020), is Labour spokesperson for Climate and Equality; and is Chairperson of the Oireachtas Special Committee on Gender Equality.

"Whatever you can do, or think you can do, do it now, boldness has genius."

GOETHE, WRITER

* * *

"In him we are bold enough to approach God in complete confidence, through our faith in him."

EPHESIANS 3:12

MY JOURNEY FROM

HOPELESSNESS TO HOPE

John O'Leary

When I was asked by my boss and line manager would I be interested in participating in this 'book of hope' by Sr Stanislaus Kennedy, I jumped at the idea. Here is my story of my journey and of what hope means to me.

I remember all those years ago when I ended up in treatment, being told whilst doing my first step and my worst drunk exercise, that I was a "hopeless case" and was probably not going to make it. It's hard to believe that twenty-five years later, by taking it a day at a time, I am no longer a hopeless case but have found hope and purpose in life. You may ask where I found that hope. Initially, I found hope by attending the Stanhope Centre in Dublin; the support I received there was life changing. Today I work as member of their team, bringing hope and guidance to others.

After treatment in Stanhope, I remember clearly carrying my worldly possessions over O'Connell Street bridge to Teach Mhuire in Gardiner Street. I was alone and uncertain of what my life would hold. As part of my journey I attended the AA meetings in Sherrard Street; sometimes attending meetings up to three times a day, still lost and wondering what to do with my life. Gradually the miracle of hope began and I grew stronger. The fog of addiction and hopelessness began to shift, and I was able to see the light at the end of the tunnel. I don't think I would be where I am today if I did not have hope, which with time and perseverance rekindled my love of life.

I have been very blessed on my journey so far; things have a way of coming together when your life is on the right path. I continue on my journey of self-discovery and to go to my recovery meetings regularly. I am currently work in the caring profession, giving back some of the goodness I have received from others. I started work in the Clancy night shelter, then did eleven years with De Paul Ireland and to date I am back to where my journey began, at the Stanhope Centre. I am reminded every day that it is about never losing hope once you have found it. It's also about doing the daily things necessary to maintain recovery, like keeping in touch with other like-minded people and remaining positive.

I would like to end with a quote:

"Never - never - ever give up on finding hope." Author unknown.

· ·

John O'Leary has spent fourteen years working in front line settings He currently works in the Stanhope Centre in Dublin as a Project Worker.

"I have learned that if we advance confidently in the direction of our dreams and endeavour to live the life we have imagined, we will meet with a success unexpected in common hours."

HENRY DAVID THOREAU, WRITER &
TRANSCENDENTALIST

* * *

"Yes, I know what plans I have in mind for you, Yahweh declares, plans for peace, not for disaster, to give you a future and a hope."

JEREMIAH 29:11

'WE LISTEN, TO KNOW WE ARE NOT ALONE'

Joseph O'Connor

I often get great hope and solace from music, not only because it is beautiful in itself, but because the desire to make it seems to come from some profound wish for empathy and connection, some zone in which we become intensely human. CS Lewis wrote: "We read to know we are not alone." I think that's also an important part of why we listen to music.

When I hear the Palestrina Choir or Aretha Franklin or Bach or Seán Ó Riada, I know that we are part of another immensity.

I have been so extraordinarily blessed to have been a husband and a father. I know very well that it's not given to everyone. The beauty, humour and kindness of my sons give me hope. They have inherited these wonderful qualities and many more from their mother, who is the most amazing person I have ever met. Some people are never done droning on about the supposed awfulness of young people, but to me the passion of the rising generation around issues of climate justice and social equality is inspiring.

Joseph O'Connor was born in Dublin in 1963. His books include the novels Ghost Light, Star of the Sea *and* Shadowplay. *He is Professor of Creative Writing at the University of Limerick.*

"*May I have the courage today*
To live the life that I would love,
To postpone my dream no longer
But do at last what I came here for
And waste my heart on fear no more."

JOHN O'DONOHUE, *TO BLESS THE SPACE BETWEEN*
US: A BOOK OF INVOCATIONS AND BLESSINGS

* * *

"*For there is a future, and your hope will*
not come to nothing."

PROVERBS 23:18

HOPE IS SUCH A SMALL WORD

Janna Majurina

Hope is such a small and yet multifaceted word! I never thought about what hope is? And now I understand how important it is to have hope for the victory of Ukraine; to believe in the courage, strength and endurance of our soldiers, and that we can again live peacefully in our land and enjoy life.

For me, hope is the realisation of my plans, wishes. I am Ukrainian, I grew up and lived in Kyiv, a flourishing and very beautiful city. I had grandiose plans for the future in my country. All this is in the past. At 5 o'clock in the morning, February 24, 2022, everything collapsed. Like a huge snowball that flies from a height with great speed, destroying everything in its path, so the war destroyed all my plans, my hopes.

With a heavy heart and with tears in my eyes, I left my beloved country, with the confidence that I would return home soon. Now I live in Ireland.

The country is beautiful; I really like it. And the people here are just wonderful; very responsive with a big, open heart. They help me, and give me hope again that everything will be fine. Hope dies last. While I live, the *hope* lives in me and I believe that I will be able to realise my new plans in the already Free Independent Ukraine. I am very grateful to the country of Ireland, which gave me and my daughter their protection during the war, as well as to the people who surround me and are always ready to lend a helping hand. Low bow to all.

. . . .

Janna Majurina or Zhanna Mazhurina is from the city of
Kyiv, Ukraine. She now lives in Inchigeelagh, Cork.

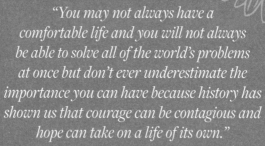

*"You may not always have a
comfortable life and you will not always
be able to solve all of the world's problems
at once but don't ever underestimate the
importance you can have because history has
shown us that courage can be contagious and
hope can take on a life of its own."*

MICHELLE OBAMA, AUTHOR & FORMER US

FIRST LADY

* * *

*"Those who are wise will shine as brightly
as the expanse of the heavens, and those
who have instructed many in uprightness,
as bright as stars for all eternity."*

DANIEL 12:3

'AS WE WAIT IN JOYFUL HOPE'

Kathleen Watkins

Live in hope.
Hope springs eternal.
I hope and pray.

I remember my Dad looking over the hedge at his cattle: "I hope they sell well," he said, "to pay for the school fees."

He was always optimistic. I am glad to say I got that from him. Hope is a positive gift. We look forward and trust that life will go well. There is always the silver lining. Miracles do happen.

All will be well. Aim high and hope for the best.
The path of life has many rocks. Fight on. Never give up.
Be a dreamer and make tomorrow better than today.

Kathleen Watkins is a well-known harpist and folk singer. She was married to the broadcaster Gay Byrne. She is also the author of the award winning picture book series for children, Pigin of Howth, *inspired by stories Kathleen told her own grandchildren.*

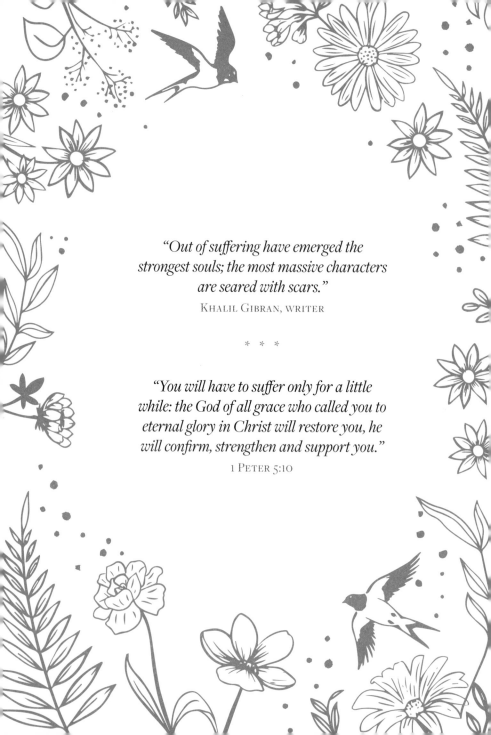

"Out of suffering have emerged the strongest souls; the most massive characters are seared with scars."

KHALIL GIBRAN, WRITER

* * *

"You will have to suffer only for a little while: the God of all grace who called you to eternal glory in Christ will restore you, he will confirm, strengthen and support you."

1 PETER 5:10

THE WARRIOR WITHIN, TURNING MY

PAIN INTO POWER

· · · · · · · · · · · · · · · · · · · ·

Kelly Ann Byrne

I am truly blessed and honoured to be asked to be a part of this collaborative book. Thank you Sister Stan.

For me in my thirty-six years of life, I have really experienced and lived through so much already. On my life's journey, from a very young age growing up in foster care - a world where I was made to feel I was a problem, that I wasn't wanted, and felt rejected and that it wasn't safe to be me - I became like a chameleon adjusting and adapting to all forms of trying to fit in, to just be accepted. That was what I felt I had to do before I had even the chance to feel my own innocence, pureness and unconditional love as a baby growing up into this world where I was projected onto from others with their pain and trauma. And because of that I believed there must have been something really wrong with me.

I have felt like I have lived a very lonely life growing up, and I began to, like a tortoise, go into my own shell where I only trusted myself. I learned how to just only survive in a form of protection mode, even though I hadn't the chance to find out who I actually was.

For me, over the years, that's where hope started to become my best friend a lot of times. I would vision in my fantasy world (mind hopes and dreams) exactly what I did want in life.

Having known all of what I didn't want, which I had experienced and still was experiencing in reality, I had this deep sense of knowing my own strength, which became stronger and stronger the more I listened to myself, and began to speak my truth.

I was always searching from very young. I didn't know what for but throughout the years I have come to find my power (my light) inside, which helped me to create my strength to overcome all life's traumas, pain and challenges; and keep going and never give up even on the days I wanted to.

I've created my mindset to look for the good in each day, some days really I have to look very hard, but I see everything as learning and growing.

I am becoming a better version of myself, who I choose to be each and every day.

One core belief of mine, that has stuck with me, is that I know I'm a good person, yes I have done wrong many a time but I've learned more through my wrongs than I have with my rights.

Hope for me is waking up each day with gratitude, wishing people well and being thankful for all that has gone well and is going well in my own life, and that of my beautiful children too. And also knowing if anything is not well, that I have the courage and strength to find ways or seek help to change it, with the hope and belief that things will get better because I am deserving of a good life. We all are; you and me. And never to take things or people for granted. By being thankful and zoning in everyday on all the good that I do have.

Even though I didn't have a physical, stable family situation growing up, I have always been connected to God and the angels, who regularly send me physical messages of hope, love and guidance. I came to understand that I never really was alone, or am ever alone, and neither are you ever.

We just need to pause and listen. Listen to our bodies, listen to our intuition and honour our feelings. Knowing we have the right to feel and think and just be ourselves.

Hope to me is a choice. With hope in my heart I still continue to keep moving forward, only ever to look back in remembrance at just how far I've travelled this journey in life and came to where I am today.

For that I am truly blessed.

Sending you all so much blessing, love, light, and hope too.

. . . .

Kelly Ann Byrne is a thirty-six-year-old warrior woman who battled through most of her life feeling so alone. She was fostered as a baby and has been in and out of homelessness throughout her life, and has suffered domestic violence. She has progressed on and pushed through all her pain with the help and support of Focus Ireland and has also become a LEAP (Lived Experience Ambassador Programme) ambassador for them, helping to prevent others from ever having to face the loneliness and trauma that she and her family have experienced, and ending homelessness for good. She has five beautiful children - two teenage boys and three beautiful girls, one of which is a twin but her twin sister passed away from cot death and is in heaven. RIP.

"*There is nothing more difficult yet more gratifying in our society than living with sincere, active, constructive hope for the human spirit.*"

MARIA POPOVA, WRITER

* * *

"*Love is always ready to make allowances, to trust, to hope and to endure whatever comes.*"

1 CORINTHIANS 13:7

HOPE REIGNS

. . . .

Liam O'Dwyer

My personal life and work life often overwhelm me. I can feel compromised by the choices I make, and work requests that mount up and need to be prioritised and dealt with. While I am aware that I am not unique in respect of these situations I feel I have let family, colleagues and friends down by being unaware of their life challenges while I focus on my own.

There is always the fear that personal circumstances cannot be repaired, and that work may get out of control leading to personal and industry exposure.

What shines a beam of light into these situations are the people who stand with you and together create the incremental changes that lead to positive outcomes be they in work or at home: The joy of the unexpected grandchildren, of an engaging family celebration, the response from colleagues who step up to the plate. Currently I see so many generous volunteers providing accommodation, money and services to people from Ukraine. I see volunteers giving their time to welcome refugees at ports and airports. The thoughtfulness of colleagues, family or friends in recognising pressure and responding with, "how can I help".

Hope is rooted in our belief about how things in life can be and in having a plan based on experience that you can move with, to a better place.

Frustration and despair is having neither a plan nor an end location – this is where others fit in. I cannot achieve either the plan nor arrive at the location (if ever) without the support of others – often as in many cases unasked for or unplanned for. I reflect on the volunteers from other organisations and some friends who assisted in our office in the early days of the Ukraine crisis, to answer the phone calls and the emails.

I often think back to my earlier days and the focus on individual development, managing alone, being stoic coupled with a belief that such stoicism would lead to a place in a kingdom of God after your journey was run – now I realise that the goal is creating this kingdom here within family, colleagues and the society we live in.

A few months after the war broke out in Ukraine I watched how a small community in Fethard, Co. Tipperary came together to provide accommodation, jobs, education and support to a group of people they had never met – the outcome is that the community in Fethard has benefited by creating a plan that delivers hope to a group of

Ukrainian people but has united their own community with a common purpose and the joy of seeing it evolve. To everyone's surprise the creativity, generosity and focus on others had a positive effect for the community in Fethard with increased employment, more children in the local schools and a sense of pride. There's no need to worry about life beyond when the kingdom of God is already here being recreated each day by generosity and co-operation.

* *

Liam O'Dwyer is the current Secretary General of the Irish Red Cross. He has worked in HR management, as a priest in the Dublin Diocese and with the Society of St Vincent de Paul, the League of Credit Unions and the Catholic Institute for Deaf people among others. Liam is married with two adult children and two grandchildren. He is passionate about soccer, and a belief that equality and access to work in society would bring hope to us all regardless of means, if only it was tried.

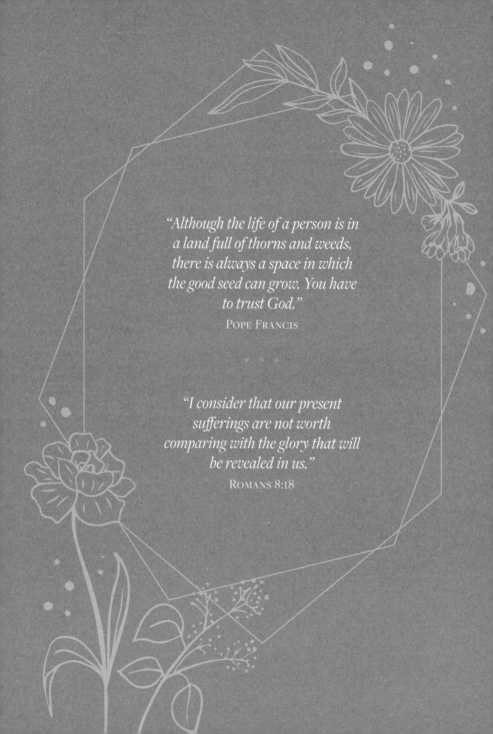

"*Although the life of a person is in a land full of thorns and weeds, there is always a space in which the good seed can grow. You have to trust God.*"

POPE FRANCIS

* * *

"*I consider that our present sufferings are not worth comparing with the glory that will be revealed in us.*"

ROMANS 8:18

RÉ AN TSOLAIS / TIME OF LIGHT

· ·

Mairéad Ní Mhaonaigh

I'm sure that my story echoes for many families during the lockdown. At the beginning of the Covid-19 pandemic my younger sister Anna Ní Mhaonaigh was diagnosed with rectal cancer. The family were all devastated to say the least, as she was always so diligent about her diet and health. She was always the strong one!

I was finding the lockdown and the lack of work hard initially, but I was just beginning to enjoy my leisure time at home with my daughter Nia; a luxury that a working, touring musician finds hard to get. We were enjoying the slowed down pace of life and this devastating news came and shook every bit of hope and joy from me. It was a difficult time to have a loved one in hospital, while not being able to visit them during their treatments but trying to be there for them. I would walk daily on empty beautiful beaches here in Carrickfinn on the North-West coast of Donegal, with only the birdsong to keep me company. This was my prayer to Anna.

The more I walked, the more I would get solace from the smallest of little things, like the sea breeze brushing my face, or the heat of the sun on my body, or the colours of the sea and sky that kept changing daily. It was sheer bliss and it lifted my spirit, and I kept giving these little joys up to Anna for her healing. As that was all I could do!

During this time I was given a commission by Patricia McBride, the director of An Grianán Theatre in Letterkenny to write some music to perform on stage in the theatre at the end of January 2021, to be broadcast online through social media.

This was a timely diversion for me. It was good for my head and for coping with what my sister was going through. So now I would lilt on my daily walk or think of lines of poetry in Gaelic to express my now growing hope for her healing. There seemed to be a glimmer of light that things were going to improve. Everyday brought a new beautiful twist to the tune or the song and gave me solace in my anxiety and worry. Eventually I named my collective compositions *Ré an tSolais* translated as the *Time of Light*.

This was all inspired by Anna, my younger sister, and her lonely journey through operations and various treatments to healing.

Below are the words of the song, which was part of the suite that I composed and performed on 24th January, 2021 in An Grianán Theatre to an empty auditorium, and subsequently shown on TG4 on St Patrick's Day 2021. (I decided to give the money generated online (€3,000) to the Donegal Hospice and the Donegal Cancer Flights and Services)

The story today is that Anna is in remission and is back working and living life to the full, embracing all the little simple joys life brings. We have all grown as a family from this experience and it has brought us closer, even though we were close prior to this.

It has made me think that having hope and believing in it is necessary for the human to survive in the darkest of days.

RÉ AN TSOLAIS

Mairéad Ní Mhaonaigh

A Ghile na Gile las solas mo chroí,
'Mo threorú go buan i nduibheagáin na h-óich'
Tá'n bealach seo corrach ach ní ghlacfaidh mé scíth
Go scroichfear ceann scríbe faoi sholas gealaí.

Tá'n oíche seo dorcha ach is feasach an tslí
'S an t-seisreach ag loinnriú i measc na réaltaí
Ach ar imeall na spéire idir dheirg dhá néal
Ó spréigheann gath gréine thar dhromchla an tsaoil.

Mar ón dubh tagann bán sin mar atá
Amhráin ársa ár sinsear, macalla na gcianta
Muna ngoilltear an duairc ní thuigtear an t- suairc
Agus guím ré an tsolais ar do chroí 's do mhianta

Coinnigh an dóchas i ndeireadh an lae
'S cóthaigh do ghrá go dtéimid sa chré
Tóg suas do mheanma ,a chara mo chléibh,
'S guím ré an tsolais ort, 's saol síochánta séimh.

TIME OF LIGHT

(Translated by my brother Gearóid Ó Maonaigh)

Bright is the brilliance that glows in my heart
And leads me my path in the gloom of this night
Along this road that is coarse, but I will not rest
Till I arrive at my destiny by this moonlight.

The night is dark but I know my way
Beneath the Plough as it radiates among the stars
Save at the brink of the sky amongst clouds of red
A sunbeam sweeps o'er the face of the Earth

After dark comes the light it's the constant way
The distant echoes of our forefathers' music
Suffer the pain to enlighten the joy
I bestow this beam to your heart's desires

In faith and in hope at the end of the day
Our love will endure 'till we return to clay
Raise up your spirits my dearest of friends
And peaceful your heart in the light of this life.

· ·

Mairéad Ní Mhaonaigh was born and raised in the Gaoth Dobhair Gaeltacht in North West Donegal. She is a native Gaelic speaker and learned her songs and tunes from her family and neighbours. Mairéad is internationally known as one of the most important fiddle players that play in the unique Donegal style. Mairéad is the lead vocalist for the Irish traditional band Altan, which she co-founded with her late husband Frankie Kennedy in 1985.

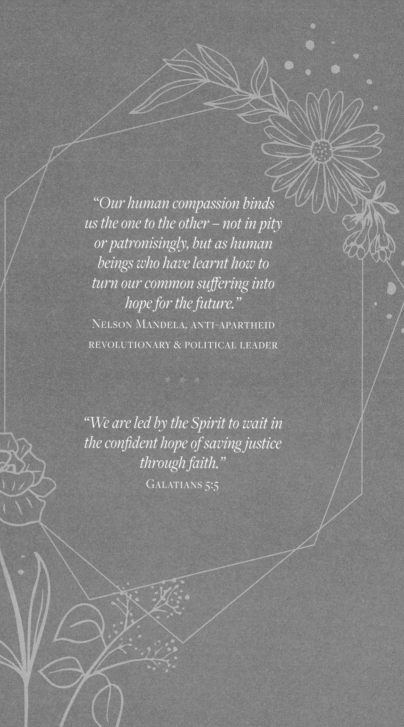

"*Our human compassion binds us the one to the other – not in pity or patronisingly, but as human beings who have learnt how to turn our common suffering into hope for the future.*"

NELSON MANDELA, ANTI-APARTHEID REVOLUTIONARY & POLITICAL LEADER

* * *

"*We are led by the Spirit to wait in the confident hope of saving justice through faith.*"

GALATIANS 5:5

TOMORROW

Marie Louise O'Donnell

Sister Mary telephoned. She asked how I was. Sister Mary looked after my mother in Holy Family Residence through her final years. My mother died in March. Sister Mary has remained a friend. The Little Sisters of the Poor are quite contemplative. But Sister Mary likes to wander around Stillorgan Shopping Centre looking in the shop windows. I bring her regularly to buy small extras for the residents on her floor. Shampoo, face creams, body lotion and Epsom salts for worn feet. We go to Dunnes and pick out coloured cardigans, soft trousers and pretty blouses. Sister Mary always knows what to buy. She matches colours, styles and patterns. The residents on her floor are very old, but everything she buys for them has vibrancy. Vibrancy for individual bodies and personal appearance.

Sister Mary says the residents love to look well. It has nothing to do with age. The residents look forward to tomorrow.

I find difficulty in writing about hope. Poets and philosophers do it so easily. And others confuse it with happiness.

Sister Mary hasn't it confused at all. Because, when she thinks about hope, she interprets it around the ordinary and the everyday.

"You have to keep going," she tells me. "That is what life is about. You just keep going."

Now when I'm asked to think about hope I immediately think of Sister Mary choosing, matching and carrying, creams, colour and style for an ageless tomorrow.

Hope is vibrancy. And smelling like spring flowers.

. . . .

Marie Louise O'Donnell is an educator,
broadcaster and writer.

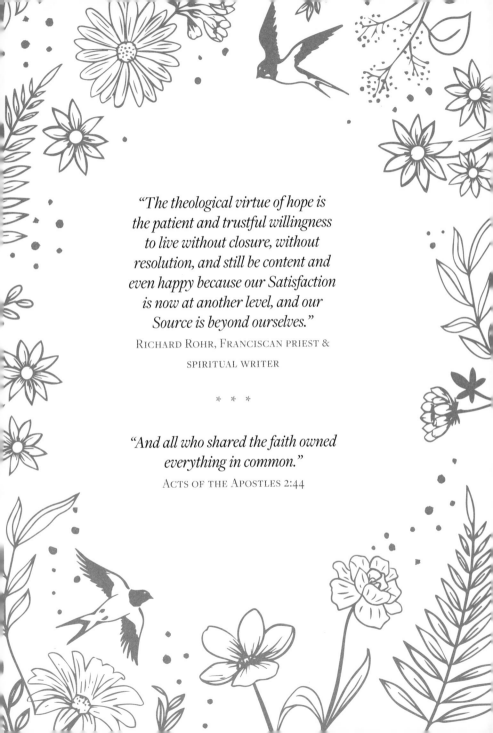

"*The theological virtue of hope is the patient and trustful willingness to live without closure, without resolution, and still be content and even happy because our Satisfaction is now at another level, and our Source is beyond ourselves.*"

RICHARD ROHR, FRANCISCAN PRIEST & SPIRITUAL WRITER

*   *   *

"*And all who shared the faith owned everything in common.*"

ACTS OF THE APOSTLES 2:44

FAITH WILL BE REWARDED

David McCullagh

It has been hard in recent times - in the face of a pandemic, of war, of environmental catastrophe - to have much hope about our future.

And yet, without hope, the temptation is to give in. Hope for a better future won't make it happen, but without hope, we certainly won't make a better future for ourselves.

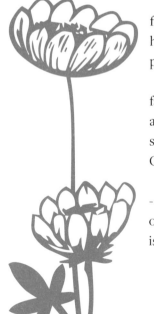

Some find hope in religion, others in their faith in humanity. And sometimes, people find hope in art or popular culture - in books, in poetry, in songs.

I remember a bleak time in the life of our family, when my wife was in hospital, seriously ill after the birth of our daughter. Every day, I would strap the baby into her car seat, and drive in to the Coombe so we could spend time with my wife.

The arrival of a first child is stressful enough - I really had *no* idea what I was doing - and obviously that is multiplied when serious illness is added to the mix.

But hope can keep you going, and in the car I

was listening over and over again to a new Bruce Springsteen CD, and particularly to the song *Land of Hope and Dreams.*

It includes a line which had particular resonance at the time: "Dreams will not be thwarted, faith will be rewarded."

As I looked down at our tiny daughter, those words filled me with hope - and thankfully that hope was justified, because my wife recovered, and our faith in the future was rewarded.

Of course, dreams sometimes *are* thwarted, and sometimes faith is *not* rewarded. But we all need to hope for a better future, because having that hope can help us build one.

David McCullagh is a journalist with RTÉ and is currently a co-presenter of the Six-One News. *He has also written five books and hopes someday to write another.*

*"I said to my soul be still
and wait without hope
For hope would be hope for the wrong
thing; wait without love
For love would be love for the wrong
thing; there is yet faith
But the faith and the love and the hope
are all in the waiting."*

T. S. Eliot, writer

* * *

*"Blessed be God the Father of our Lord
Jesus Christ, who in his great mercy has
given us a new birth into a living hope
through the resurrection of Jesus Christ
from the dead and into a heritage that
can never be spoilt or soiled
and never fade away."*

1 Peter 1:3-4

HISTORY IS MY HOPE

. . . .

Mary Kenny

W hat gives me hope is history. Human beings are flawed – I agree with what I learned in my Penny Catechism about our tendency to err and fail – and yet we learn by our mistakes, and we try to correct them.

History is a series of corrections, if sometimes over-corrections, but there's always that effort to do better. We engage in violent war and persecutions, but then we seek to reconcile, to make peace, and to make amends to victims of these depredations. Sometimes this reaction becomes excessive or disproportionate, as when a revulsion against slavery means arbitrarily destroying every link having the remotest connection with the slave trade – Gladstone, a decent Christian, has had his reputation attacked because of a tenuous family association, which wasn't his fault. But 'going too far' is part of the process of highlighting a wrong previously under-emphasised.

Liberation movements seek to free people from the fetters of over-rigid systems of control – sometimes, again, in excess. Women's liberation was a necessary movement for female emancipation, but some men now feel that women are over-favoured, given professional positions for token reasons, and accorded more privilege in cases such as disputed custody of children. But such social tendencies, if they exist, are a compensatory balancing of past prejudices when women were denied job positions, or fathers were regarded as the primary family guardians. The feminist claim that we must 'believe all women' doesn't always hold true – women, being human, are quite capable of uttering falsehoods – but the claim was a necessary counterpoint to a previous notion that women's statements weren't to be taken seriously.

We live and learn. We correct and sometimes over-correct. We examine where we have gone wrong, personally and collectively. That gives me hope that eventually we arrive at truth and balance.

. . . .

Mary Kenny is a veteran journalist and writer who has contributed to over thirty-five publications in Ireland, Britain, the US, and, unexpectedly, Norway. Her book on Catholic Ireland since 1922, The Way We Were, *was published by Columba Books in August 2022. See www.mary-kenny.com*

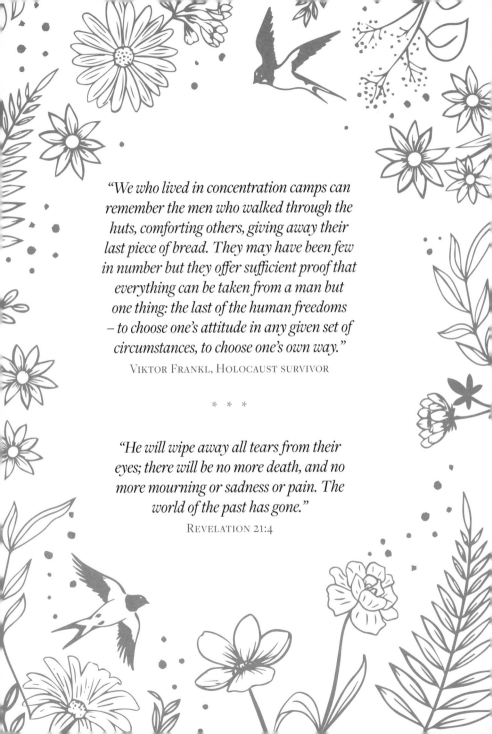

"We who lived in concentration camps can remember the men who walked through the huts, comforting others, giving away their last piece of bread. They may have been few in number but they offer sufficient proof that everything can be taken from a man but one thing: the last of the human freedoms – to choose one's attitude in any given set of circumstances, to choose one's own way."

VIKTOR FRANKL, HOLOCAUST SURVIVOR

* * *

"He will wipe away all tears from their eyes; there will be no more death, and no more mourning or sadness or pain. The world of the past has gone."

REVELATION 21:4

THE GOODNESS OF PEOPLE

Taoiseach Micheál Martin

The most common source of hope for me in my everyday life is the fundamental goodness of people.

I'm fortunate to get the chance to see it in many aspects of life throughout the State, but perhaps never more so than in the genuinely extraordinary response of the Irish people to the humanitarian crisis caused by Russia's invasion of Ukraine.

In every corner of the country, people have opened their communities, their homes and their hearts to women and children forced onto the road by this cruel war.

Another thing that gives me hope daily are my interactions with the committed and idealistic young people in our country.

Their passion for their country and the world around them is a very powerful force for positive change. When I stood on the steps of Government Buildings in December 2021 and told the country about the need for more restrictions, I spoke directly to our children and young people and thanked them for their efforts. I described them as a very special generation.

That was before they too stepped up and put their arms around our new Ukrainian friends in their social circles, in their families, and on our sports fields.

And it is sport which has given me hope and inspiration throughout my life. The simple joy of the endeavour, the engagement with supporters, the perspective and balance that it brings people; sport is a thread that binds so many within our communities and binds us all together as a nation.

It has given me some of my best days and been a constant in some of the worst.

In our first century as a State, we have been through a lot. And while we face many significant and important challenges today, our social and economic progress has been incredible.

When I look back at the journey we have made, it is clear that these themes of our country's common goodness, our talented youth, and the closeness and solidarity of our communities have played a huge role in our success.

When I look forward, I have no doubt that they will continue to sustain us and unlock more and more potential in the time ahead.

· ·

Micheál Martin is Taoiseach, leader of Fianna Fáil and TD for Cork South Central.

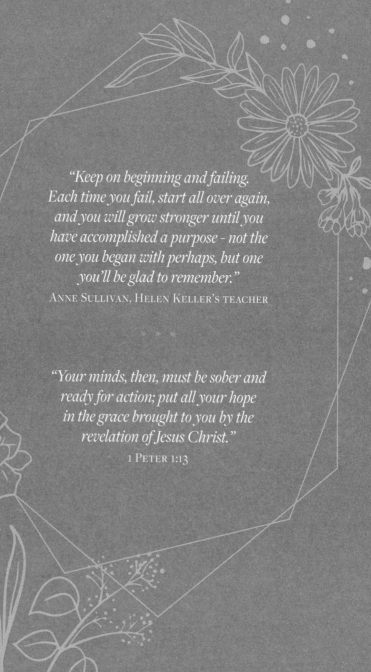

"*Keep on beginning and failing.
Each time you fail, start all over again,
and you will grow stronger until you
have accomplished a purpose - not the
one you began with perhaps, but one
you'll be glad to remember.*"

ANNE SULLIVAN, HELEN KELLER'S TEACHER

* * *

"*Your minds, then, must be sober and
ready for action; put all your hope
in the grace brought to you by the
revelation of Jesus Christ.*"

1 PETER 1:13

HOPE AS RESPONSIBILITY

· ·

Moya Doherty

H ope is not the same thing as optimism, with which it is often aligned. Optimism is a luxury available only to those who can see a future for themselves. Hope resides in another space, one where, rather than being seen as an emotion, it becomes an energy, a conviction that despite the present circumstances, ultimately truth will make sense however that sense turns out. It is unfortunate that in recent times the behaviour of those deemed capable of leading, combined with natural threats such as climate change and viral pandemic, have eroded our capacity for such hope. The greatest hope lies in the capacity of the human soul for creative expression. As Yeats said, "We make out of the quarrel with others, rhetoric, but of the quarrel with ourselves, poetry," and it is in this creative quarrel that the seeds of hope remain, a creative latency ready for the moment when Heaney's hope and reason rhyme. Hope will be constructed on a foundation of science, technology and art where science brings knowledge through experiment, technology creates possibilities and art brings meaning. It is the responsibility of those with a public voice to challenge the apparent inevitability of poverty, conflict, discrimination, inequality and to argue for a social, economic and cultural environment grounded in the concept of hope and care for one another. By so doing, and by constructing an alternative form of collective citizenship, it becomes possible to move the debate from the public to the personal and to allow oneself to again believe in the power of hope to change one's personal life for the better and to build a future worthy of the hope invested in it.

. . . .

Moya Doherty is a producer, creative executive and creative futures advocate.

"Most of the important things in the world have been accomplished by people who have kept on trying when there seemed to be no hope at all."

DALE CARNEGIE, WRITER

* * *

"May our Lord Jesus Christ himself, and God our Father who has given us his love and, through his grace, such ceaseless encouragement and such sure hope, encourage you and strengthen you in every good word and deed."

2 THESSALONIANS 2:16-17

WHAT IS HOPE?

. . . .

Myles Dungan

H ope is what Marilyn Monroe wrote three times on the back of her wedding photograph. So, that's probably not a good place to start.

"Hope deferred maketh the something sick."

No! Me neither!

Apparently, Vladimir (Didi) says it in Beckett's *Waiting for Godot* and it does sound like something he or Estragon would say. I always thought it was an enigmatic line from Gertrude Stein. I have no idea where that notion came from.

A few minutes research reveals that Didi was struggling to remember a line from the Bible, Proverbs 13:12 to be precise. "Hope deferred maketh the heart sick but a desire fulfilled is a tree of life."

Can you conjure hope? Not the Didi sort of hope, where he and Estragon are just waiting around for someone else to arrive and release them from their existential angst and spellbinding boredom. While the hell that is supposed to be 'other people' can clearly influence the water levels in our reservoir of hope, it's better to think of it as a self-generating sort of thing.

A wise man once told me - an Irish Olympic rower actually (Hi Nev!)—that we can *decide* to be positive or negative. Even though I was more than a decade older than him and, therefore, supposedly wiser, I'd never framed it in that way before. The more I thought about it the more I realised that he was right.

Glass half empty or half full? It's really up to you. And what is 'hope' if not a single-syllable thesaurus alternative for positivity.

So, don't hang about waiting for your particular Godot. The chances are that only Pozzo and Lucky will turn up. Conjure up that proverbial 'tree of life' for yourself.

Myles Dungan is a writer and broadcaster. The author of more than a dozen books on Irish and American history, he is the presenter of the RTÉ Radio 1 programme The History Show. *When he grows up (finally) he wants to write detective novels or be a cross between Terry Pratchett and P.G. Wodehouse.*

"Life is beautiful to me and worth living and full of meaning. Despite everything."

ETTY HILLESUM, WRITER & HOLOCAUST VICTIM

* * *

"As for me, my hope will never fade, I will praise you more and more."

PSALMS 71:14

HOPE FOR A FUTURE WORTH

HOPING FOR

· · · · · · · · · · · · · · ·

Niall Leahy

As a nation we have never eaten, drunk, dressed, driven or holidayed as well as we have in the last forty years. We, myself included, have enthusiastically chased every luxury available to us. Question: has this time of consumer optimism been a time of real hope? I am inclined to say no.

An important characteristic of hope is that it hopes for something worth hoping for. You can't hope for bad health or a fleeting pleasure that will ultimately make you miserable. It is now clear that our years of buoyant shopping have left us in a precarious situation - ecologically, economically, socially and spiritually. It is impossible to hope for a lifestyle that is incompatible with life itself.

Hope is reborn when you press the reset button and set your sights on a future actually worth hoping for. Thanks be to God many people are doing this and we can already see in the present many signs that are pointing to a new future. These signs give me hope: a friend ordering vegetarian; colleagues opting for the train instead of the plane; keeping the grass down by inviting the local school children to play in our garden; our homegrown tomatoes and strawberries tasting so good; our politicians passing climate laws.

Is all this too little too late? Maybe. But if you want to live in hope, then I suggest setting your hopes on people rather than predictions; people who are choosing life over lifestyle. Because when it comes down to it, the question is not 'what gives you hope?' but 'who gives you hope?' The risen Jesus is one such person, so if you are short on hope I invite you to join me in this simple prayer, "Lord Jesus, give me hope".

. . . .

Fr Niall Leahy SJ is a Jesuit priest based in Gardiner Street Parish, Dublin and a contributor to the podcast Sons of Ignatius.

"In the stillness of the quiet, if we listen, we can hear the whisper of the heart giving strength to weakness, courage to fear, hope to despair."

HOWARD THURMAN, WRITER & CIVIL RIGHTS ACTIVIST

* * *

"Be brave, take heart, all who put your hope in Yahweh."

PSALMS 31:24

THE METAMORPHOSIS OF NJABULO —

VICTIM TO SURVIVOR

. . . .

Nompumelelo Mnyandu (Njabulo)

Hope for me was when I saw the plane ticket in my hands.
Hope was when customs stamped my passport and let me through.

Hope was when the plane flew off.

Hope was when the plane landed safely in Ireland.

Hope for me was when I entered Ireland and started the asylum process.

Hope was seeing buildings and buses with LGBTQ+ flags flying because the previous month had been Pride Month.

Hope was and continues to be in LGBT Ireland Is Rainbow Muid [support group].

Hope is the continued support from the Lisdoonvarna community.

Hope was having the courage of coming out as a transman and being accepted.

Hope is waking up every day with no fear, having a secure job and being able to give back to the community in any way I can.

Hope was having a safe place to sleep, being included in public consultations on issues that impacted everyone collectively, being invited to public platforms to share and give light to situations that are mostly hidden to the rest of the world, being given a voice.

To leave home, the only place you have ever known, to leave your family, friends, colleagues, culture, food and your way of living, is the most painful and traumatic situation one can find themselves in. To embark on a journey of no return, to get to your destination and to adapt takes a lot of courage and resilience. This would otherwise prove very difficult in the absence of hope. Hope that has been brought by the different Irish Citizens I have encountered for totally different reasons. Hope that came from the freedom of expression, the acceptance of diversity, the inclusiveness that Ireland strives to live up to everyday. Hope has been everyone that works tirelessly for human rights, against homophobia and just general equality of all human beings. Hope has been my metamorphosis, from being a victim to being a survivor and hope for others.

. . . .

Nompumelelo Mnyandu, who prefers Njabulo, is originally from South Africa but is now based in Lisdoonvarna, Co. Clare; passionate about LGBTQ+ equality and rights both in a workspace and within the community; Ernst & Young Employee; a member of Is Rainbow Muid and co-founder of Quare Clare.

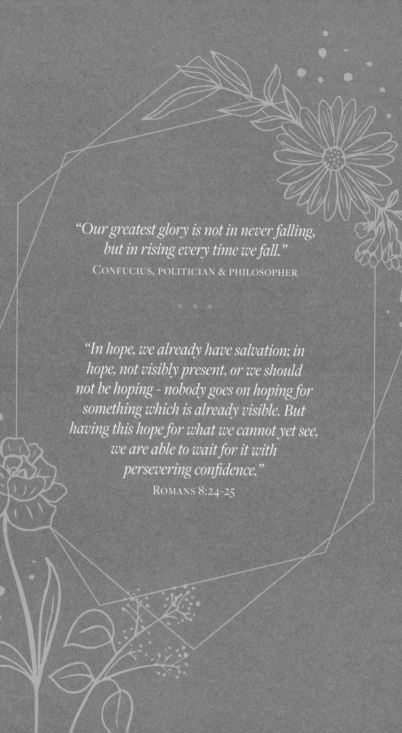

"*Our greatest glory is not in never falling,
but in rising every time we fall.*"
CONFUCIUS, POLITICIAN & PHILOSOPHER

* * *

"*In hope, we already have salvation; in
hope, not visibly present, or we should
not be hoping - nobody goes on hoping for
something which is already visible. But
having this hope for what we cannot yet see,
we are able to wait for it with
persevering confidence.*"
ROMANS 8:24-25

A THING WITH FEATHERS

Sharon Ní Bheoláin

Hope is the thing with feathers
    That perches in the soul,
      And sings the tune without the words,
      And never stops at all,
And sweetest in the gale is heard;
      And sore must be the storm
      That could abash the little bird
      That kept so many warm.
I've heard it in the chillest land,
      And on the strangest sea;
      Yet, never, in extremity,
      It asked a crumb of me.

Emily Dickinson was disinclined to give her poems titles; I like to think she preferred her work to be interpreted beyond mere words on a page. In this variously numbered poem (254 or 314) the enigmatic and famously reclusive writer conjures up a vivid and curiously comforting metaphor; one which I like to visualise in times of despair.

Hope is a bird; an irrepressible energy perched in the soul of each and every one of us, it sustains us even in the "chillest land" and "strangest sea" with its endless, wordless song.

Is that not the very definition of 'hope'; an ever-present (I like to imagine brightly-plumaged) life force that resides within each one of us? It's innate, untaught, not influenced by wealth or stature and in those dark, bleak times that cast a shadow, one which won't be out run, our very own bird is singing at its "sweetest" and willing us to go on.

Dickinson is emphatic; hope is "the thing with feathers". Think about it; feathers are luxuriously soft and comforting to the touch, they are also insulating and in the avian world they are an instrument of communication. Reaching out and communing with those with whom we are close, is the single most important thing we can do when things seem to conspire against us and life feels hopeless.

Critically, feathers facilitate flight; in times of apparent desolation this "thing with feathers" called hope allows our mind to soar far beyond that place of despair to a place of light.

We need always to draw on hope. Hope for ourselves, our families, our communities and our planet. We need always to tap into that enduring song within, wordless but still full of meaning.

• •

Sharon Ní Bheoláin is a TV anchor/presenter with RTÉ.
She has worked in a variety of roles across the organisation
covering, news, politics and the monthly edition of Crimecall.

"Far away there in the sunshine are my highest aspirations. I may not reach them, but I can look up and see their beauty, believe in them, and try to follow where they lead."

LOUISA MAY ALCOTT, WRITER

* * *

"We are subjected to every kind of hardship, but never distressed; we see no way out but we never despair; we are pursued but never cut off; knocked down, but still have some life in us; always we carry with us in our body the death of Jesus so that the life of Jesus, too, may be visible in our body."

2 CORINTHIANS 4:8-10

THREE DAILY RITUALS OF HOPE

Tim Kearney

Why is it that we can so easily lose hope in our daily lives? Is it because of the pervading sense of angst and hopelessness in our divided, unequal and over-heating world? Or because of our innate human condition which tends to focus on the negative voices which are the loudest in our social media, and often in our own minds and hearts? In my own life in this fast-moving yet fragile world of ours, I have three daily rituals which help to keep me centred and which renew in me a sense of hope.

The first is the practice of interiority. Be it taking some time to slow down and reflect, or to just be still, or to read a sacred text and pray, I am led inwards to where I can connect again with the mystery and meaning of my life.

The second is the practice of a daily walk, as often as possible in green areas or in nature. I am fortunate to live beside a huge forest in France which has a wonderful biodiversity of trees and species. Walking, as Gandhi reminds us, is a great way to manage our stress and even more so when walking in the beauty of nature.

The third is the practice of presence, simply taking the time to 'be present' to family and friends; my wife, Maria; our four wonderful children; and my fellow travellers in L'Arche with whom I share community life,

especially those with an intellectual disability, who remind me each day of the importance of friendship.

By nature, I tend to move too fast and to do too much. My family and friends call me to slow down, to reconnect and 'to be' in the present moment.

Hope, which is an attitude of trust in the future, comes from being grounded in the grace of the present, and having faith in 'the other', both human and divine.

. . . .

Tim Kearney is the current director of La Ferme,
an international spiritual centre in France, and a
L'Arche community based on a life of interiority and
hospitality to people of all faiths and none.

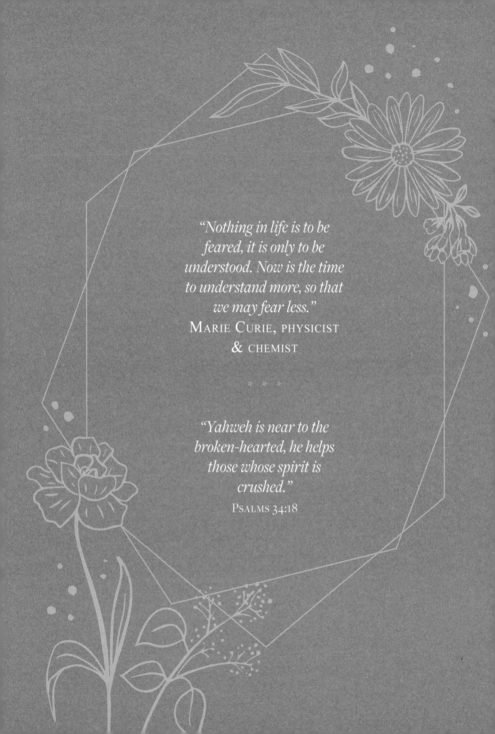

"Nothing in life is to be feared, it is only to be understood. Now is the time to understand more, so that we may fear less."
MARIE CURIE, PHYSICIST
& CHEMIST

* * *

"Yahweh is near to the broken-hearted, he helps those whose spirit is crushed."
PSALMS 34:18

SERVING PEOPLE BRINGS HOPE TO

YOURSELF AND OTHERS

Paul Reid

My role carries a lot of responsibilities and is often quite public. This I regard as a privilege. But as a public service role the job can sometimes be the subject of much public commentary and indeed criticism.

I use many techniques and practices to ensure that I understand some of the criticism but don't get absorbed by it. This involves being conscious of what gives me hope in my life and not just in a work context.

I really enjoy having the great opportunity to 'serve' people. I remind myself of this every day. No matter how tough a workday may be, or a challenge that I'm working on, I always try to stand back and remind myself that when this challenge is resolved or a matter overcome that someone, somewhere, over time, will benefit. This is what public service is all about.

One simple act of kindness, that I experience each day, outweighs acts of negativity by a factor of ten. Well at least that's what I remind myself! I avoid taking social media too seriously. For every hundred negative comments that may be referenced about me or my role, I receive at least ten nice pieces of correspondence or cards to my office, thanking us for what we do. There is much more positive energy expended by people in writing and sending a card, than the seconds it takes to write negativity on social media.

Being honest, humble and grounded also provides me with daily learning. I find that learning in my life and work makes me a better person. Being a better person provides me with great hope for the future.

Finally, a call from wife and family or a daily picture of my granddaughter in Texas, USA, provides me with great inspiration.

* *

Paul Reid has led many organisations in the private, not-for-profit, central and local governments; most recently as CEO of the HSE. He was born and reared in Finglas West and left school at the age of sixteen. He is married with two grown up children and one granddaughter.

*"We are stronger, gentler, more resilient,
and more beautiful than
any of us imagine."*

MARK NEPO, POET & PHILOSOPHER

✳ ✳ ✳

*"Put your hope in Yahweh, be strong, let
your heart be bold, put your hope
in Yahweh."*

PSALMS 27:14

THIS POEM IS A ZONE OF SANCTUARY -

FOR MARY CRILLY

Paula Meehan

It is old as the fates the stars above spin
Night after night on the face of the heavens
Endlessly telling each other their stories.

It is newborn each day with its latest version.
It says: come forward to childhood, to be cradled,
To be dandled, to be held, to be lulled.

It falls like rain to parched earth; it fires the seed
That waits with patience for its moment to open.
It says: you are worthy, deserving of love.

This poem is a zone of sanctuary:
It will speak the unspeakable. It promises a language
To bind body to soul. Its business is truth. Its business is justice.

It holds these words as a solemn promise
To those shackled in hells of earthly torment.
It will carry your witness, a cherished gift.

It opens its doors to all who need shelter.
It is humbled by your courage when you cross the threshold.
It takes your hand: it unclenches your fist finger by finger.

It opens to the light the lines of your future
That channel your energy to make yourself whole.
This poem is a zone of sanctuary.

Its words are refuge from the abusers of words.
If it says river sky star street it means river sky star street.
It means exactly what it says and says exactly what it means.

It restores to words their ancient dignities.
Though the world may be blind and deaf to your suffering
It hears you. It sees you.

It knows that the child deep inside feels defiled
With every outrage, predation or plunder,
With every transgression of their bodily form.

It reminds you again of your magnificent wildness,
That you move in grace, a creature of nature,
Hardwired to survive. Its garden is boundless.

Come rest in its shelter, sleep safe in its shade.
Look — the day moon mirrored in its pool!
Look — the seedlings in patterns, their colours radiant!

This poem honours your birthright. It honours the guardians
Who defend and vindicate this inviolate space.
This poem is a zone of sanctuary.

This poem was written to mark the granting of the Freedom of the City of Cork to Mary Crilly on the 9th June 2022. Mary was one of the founders of the Cork Rape Crisis Centre back in 1983 and is CEO of the Sexual Violence Centre. She accepted the Freedom on behalf of the more than 10,000 men, women and children who came through their doors, and the people who held out a hand to them. Mary Crilly and citizens like her give me hope.

Paula Meehan is an Irish poet and playwright.

"My great hope is to laugh as much as I cry; to get my work done and try to love somebody and have the courage to accept the love in return."

MAYA ANGELOU, POET & CIVIL RIGHTS ACTIVIST

* * *

"May the God of hope fill you with all joy and peace in your faith, so that in the power of the Holy Spirit you may be rich in hope."

ROMANS 15:13

EYE TO EYE

. . . .

Pauline Bewick

Hope for me is really large, it has a large significance, or very small. When I say very small I mean – "I hope there is jam on the tray", whereas it could also be "I hope there is not going to be a war in this country", it can be huge or it can be tiny. In a way, hope is a very useful emotion and at the same time I don't think we should depend on it altogether

I think hope comes into our everyday thinking, our everyday language with all people and all moments, it is a very overused word. It is not thought through very much, so for instance you'd say I hope it doesn't rain, but that's a frivolous thing to say really because it is not going to make any difference whether it rains or not by saying the word hope.

Hope can be used in so many different levels, it is a very useful and comforting word when it comes to saying "I hope that someone is not too ill or not suffering too much", it's truly heart felt, therefore it means something to the person that uses that word 'Hope'.

Sister Stan's advice to me a long time ago was when a homeless person is begging and you have no money to give, eye contact means more than dropping money in the hat. Eye contact is much more important as from that glimpse to each other it gives a huge amount of hope; it is a natural human greeting and the feeling lasts longer, its acknowledgement.

If one had a day of being on the street and nobody gave you eye contact you would end up being very unhappy and if there was no money in the hat and eye contact was shared then that day would not feel empty.

. . . .

One of Ireland's more acclaimed artists, Pauline Bewick was raised on a small farm in Co. Kerry. Her mother Harry brought her two daughters to Ireland in the late 30s leaving Northumberland, England. Following their time in Kerry, they went on to live in Wales and then England once again, moving from progressive school to school, living in a caravan, a houseboat, a railway carriage, a workman's hut, a gate lodge and, later in a Dublin city house. Bewick started to paint at the age of two and continued throughout her life. On turning 70, Pauline donated 500 pieces of her life's work to the Irish Nation. The Seven Ages Collection represents each decade and facet of a woman's life and is permanently on display in Waterford and Kerry.

This piece was completed by Pauline Bewick before her untimely death in June 2022.

"*Truly, it is in the darkness that one finds the light, so when we are in sorrow, then this light is nearest of all to us.*"

MEISTER ECKHART, THEOLOGIAN,

PHILOSOPHER & MYSTIC

* * *

"*Though hardships without number beset the upright, Yahweh brings rescue from them all.*"

PSALMS 34:19

THERE IS NO POINT HOPING FOR A BETTER PAST

· · · · · · · · · · · ·

Philip King

W hen I come back home to Cork City and I walk down Washington St, the juke box in my head is whirring. The music and the songs that were dropped into my ear as a boy are playing, collapsing time and bringing me right back to my childhood, gripping my father's hand as we walk toward the Capitol Cinema just after Christmas.

Here I am again, full of innocence and wonder, and hope for the future.

This was the beginning; this was where I fell into the place, where everything is music (see below).

It's been an ongoing, marvellous and miraculous expedition ever since, with hope and creativity at its heart and at its soul.

Now creativity is a complex bundle of many things and those of us who work in this world understand exactly what that means: we live with very high levels of uncertainty and access to relatively limited and sporadic resources; we understand the concept of job security but it does not really apply to us, we are gig economy veterans; we are resourceful, agile, adaptable, opportunistic; we need to be good at making a little go a long way; we need to be expert at finding creative approaches to solving problems; we understand collaboration and cooperation; we embrace diversity; we challenge; we fail; we excel; we are vulnerable; we are missing a layer of skin and we're motivated to keep going.

One of the most important things we do is that we create new things, new dreams, new ways of seeing and thinking and doing.

Hope is the key.

Hope is the fuel that keeps us keeping on ...

Hope is thing that lets us know that everything will be all right no matter how it turns out. And of course there is no point hoping for a better past.

Where Everything is Music
Don't worry about saving these songs!
And if one of our instruments breaks,
it doesn't matter.
We have fallen into the place
where everything is music.
The strumming and the flute notes
rise into the atmosphere,
and even if the whole world's harp
should burn up, there will still be
hidden instruments playing.
So the candle flickers and goes out.
We have a piece of flint, and a spark.
This singing art is sea foam.
The graceful movements come from a pearl
somewhere on the ocean floor.

Poems reach up like spindrift and the edge
of driftwood along the beach, wanting!
They derive
from a slow and powerful root
that we can't see.
Stop the words now.
Open the window in the centre of your chest,
and let the spirits fly in and out.

RUMI

· ·

*Philip King, co-founder of South Wind Blows, is a curator
and producer of bespoke cultural events. In 1987, with
writer and director Nuala O'Connor, he produced the
ground-breaking and award-winning series* Bringing It
All Back Home – the story of Irish Music and America.
*In 1993 Philip was nominated for a Grammy for his music
documentary* Rocky World, *about the Canadian musician
Daniel Lanois. He continues to produce and direct film,
television and cultural events. Most notably, Philip co-
created Ireland's best-known music series,* Other Voices,
with Oscar-winning musician Glen Hansard.

"I don't think of all the misery, but
of the beauty that still remains."

Anne Frank,

diarist & Holocaust victim

* * *

"For the needy is not forgotten for ever, not
for ever does the hope of the poor
come to nothing."

Psalm 9:18

LIFE

· · · · · ·

Proinnsias Ó Duinn

Since Homo sapiens arrived on Earth, the human animal has proven to be, in equal parts, the most destructive and creative creature on the planet. History documents in detail the extent of man's inhumanity to man. Equally, we have evidence of man's extraordinary kindness, sympathy and empathy in times of emergencies or disaster. Unfortunately, in this age of multi- media communication and twenty-four-hour visual news-broadcasting, the most effective headlines tend to be of bad news and tragedies. "No news is good news," is all too often, "Good news is no news". At every turn we are constantly bombarded with negativity and advertisements informing us of everything we must have and seldom what we actually need.

In all of this *mélange* it is too easy to be overwhelmed and lose sight of the wonders of the age in which we live. A child today at three years of age, has more information at his or her disposal than

Aristotle had in his lifetime. The trick is to learn to understand it and use it to our benefit.

So where does 'hope' come into all of this? At any time, or in any activity, we automatically 'hope' or 'wish' for a satisfactory outcome. In itself these words are aspirational and mean little unless they are backed by focused action. I recall a horologist responding to a frustrated customer who said he had great faith in his watch which wasn't working. He answered "faith/hope without good works doesn't mean a thing".

I accept that I have been fortunate and privileged to spend my life recreating, with the sensitive collective minds and talents of musicians, the creative work of some of the world's greatest composers. The atmosphere is always positive, and the strength of the collective concentration is powerful. We study and rehearse together in order to relive for the audience the intentions and spirit of some of the most inspired creative artistic minds in the history of mankind.

Does everyone in an audience listening appreciate the extent of this preparation? Not necessarily, but that is not the issue. Our task and responsibility is to endeavour to recreate it to the best of our ability. We owe that to everyone and to that end, we 'hope', 'wish', 'pray', nothing unforetold happens to deflect us from achieving this. Have enough of us learned to relax and listen to beautiful music? As individuals, how often do we stop and listen to the bird's morning chorus in spring, or actually observe and appreciate the spectacular wonders provided by nature. We only have to clear our minds, listen and observe.

We are constantly challenged throughout our lives. It is a sad situation if attempted solutions are not backed by 'hope'. It is equally sad, however, if 'hope' is not supported by solutions. Many philosophies teach us positive ways forward in this short life on earth. The ones that attract me most are those that ask us to face reality without bitterness, take personal responsibility for our actions and address life and its problems with a positive attitude. Without underlying hope or positive thinking, it must be very difficult to strive for change in ourselves, or in the circumstances in which we live.

· ·

In his early career Proinnsías Ó Duinn was a cellist. He later became Conductor of the RTÉ Chamber Choir and Vocal Adviser to Irish Radio and Television. During this period, he was a regular guest with the BBC orchestras. He went on to accept the position of Principal Conductor of the RTÉ Concert Orchestra, a role he held for twenty-five years. In 2003 he became the first Conductor Laureate to be appointed in the history of the Irish Radio/Television and was appointed to the Board of Directors of the Contemporary Music Centre of Ireland. In 2006 he was commissioned by the Royal Dublin Society to make a new edition of Benedict's opera The Lilly of Killarney. *Since 1979 he has been Conductor and Music Director of Our Lady's Choral Society.*

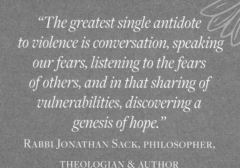

"*The greatest single antidote
to violence is conversation, speaking
our fears, listening to the fears
of others, and in that sharing of
vulnerabilities, discovering a
genesis of hope.*"

RABBI JONATHAN SACK, PHILOSOPHER,

THEOLOGIAN & AUTHOR

* * *

"*Why be so downcast, why all these
sighs? Hope in God! I will praise him
still, my Saviour, my God. When I
am downcast I think of you: from the
land of Jordan and Hermon, I think
of you, humble mountain.*"

PSALMS 42:5-6

THE WORD OF THE DAY IS HOPE

Ray Kennedy

Hope, while a small word, is one of the most powerful challenges laid down to us by the English language. It is also one of the most sought-after thoughts in our daily lives, which can change in an instant. The word 'hope' can be lengthened to mean failure when it becomes the word 'hopeless' - or mourned when it becomes a 'hoped' for thing that was just out of reach and slipped from our grasp as our 'hope' turned to 'dismay'.

But hope, as a feeling, can be the most powerful of all. It is the thought of hope and finding it in the most difficult of times - when you'll need it most. I have found and observed hope and despair residing beside each other and in a duel against each other around the world.

I've been to the scenes of great natural disasters and terrorist attacks and wars, which I've covered as a journalist. I've travelled across Africa during civil war and famine. Hope and despair are found in equal measure at times.

There was little hope in Thailand in 2005 when I was reporting from the Asian Tsunami, when thousands upon thousands died. Every day new photos were placed at the town hall in Phuket for missing children, never to be found. And yet, as townspeople brought food and warmth to the survivors, hope made me shed a tear, as I often do when I think back on those days.

Despair can easily be found all over our troubled globe, but as we survey the horror of war and famine, what we do to help each other and put an arm around a fellow man or woman while saying the simplest of sentences - "everything will be ok" - means hope is always there too.

For some it can perhaps sound hollow. However, as an action, hope can be found everywhere. In our darkest day, in our worst hour, a hand will always reach out to you and you can reach out to touch that hand. The sun will come up, the planet will spin and that most powerful of words - 'hope'- will be heard by us again and again; once we listen and wish to hear it.

. . . .

Ray Kennedy has been a journalist for over thirty years and is currently a news presenter with RTÉ. An award-winning journalist, he has also worked with Sky News and many other radio and newspaper media outlets. He has specialised in covering international affairs and hold BA degrees in both Law and International Relations.

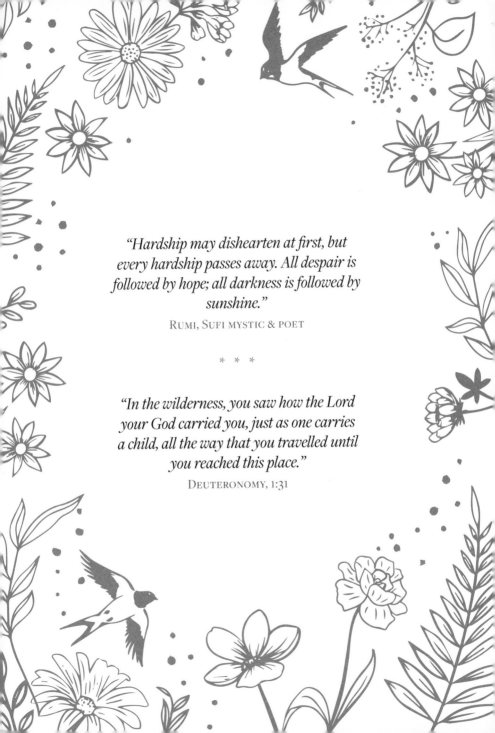

"Hardship may dishearten at first, but every hardship passes away. All despair is followed by hope; all darkness is followed by sunshine."

RUMI, SUFI MYSTIC & POET

* * *

"In the wilderness, you saw how the Lord your God carried you, just as one carries a child, all the way that you travelled until you reached this place."

DEUTERONOMY, 1:31

TO LIVE, ONE MUST BREATHE AND HOPE

Rhona Mahony

The Oxford dictionary defines hope as "to want something to happen and think that it is possible". This is a proper and concise definition but it is odd to me to see such an enormous glorious feeling described in such ordinary terms. I appreciate that hope is a small word that you might easily pass on a page, but this smallness belies a gigantic boldness that can defy the very worst things that life can conjure.

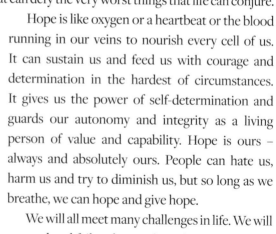

Hope is like oxygen or a heartbeat or the blood running in our veins to nourish every cell of us. It can sustain us and feed us with courage and determination in the hardest of circumstances. It gives us the power of self-determination and guards our autonomy and integrity as a living person of value and capability. Hope is ours – always and absolutely ours. People can hate us, harm us and try to diminish us, but so long as we breathe, we can hope and give hope.

We will all meet many challenges in life. We will succeed and fail and struggle and soar. There will be dreadful days when solutions feel very far away and wonderful days when dreams feel very close.

On the darkest days we might feel deserted by people and places and hope. On the brightest days, we will brim with hope as we step forward into sought-after futures full of people and places we love. On all of these days, brilliant and awful, hope is constant; reassuring us that we can endure because tomorrow will be better. On all of these days, we can give hope to others through acts of kindness and compassion that make this day better.

· ·

Dr Rhona Mahony is an obstetrician, Eisenhower Fellow and Previous Master of the National Maternity Hospital.

"There are moments in our lives when we are called to stand at the edge, where the possibilities before us are immense, the challenges mighty. These moments call for creativity, courage and hope."

Sʀ Sᴛᴀɴ, ꜱᴏᴄɪᴀʟ ᴀᴄᴛɪᴠɪꜱᴛ & ᴀᴜᴛʜᴏʀ

* * *

"Be joyful in hope, persevere in hardship; keep praying regularly."

Rᴏᴍᴀɴꜱ 12:12

POETICS OF HOPE

. . . .

Richard Kearney

Opening a door and hoping grace may enter your life. Simple as that. We do it every day. The Irish verb for hoping – *tá súil amach agam ort* – says it all: I have an eye out for you. Or the common greeting: *Fáilte roimh torann do chos, ní amháin tú fhéin* - even before yourself arrives, the echo of your footstep is music to my ears.

Hope as listening, imagining, attending, expecting. It's spiritual as well as physical. As when Yahweh promises the people – "I am who may be if you let me be" (Exodus 3: 14). Which Augustine renders colloquially as: "In the word God is contained everything we hope for."

Life waiting for us as we wait for life. A mutual anticipation associated with the renewal of spring. Light returning after darkness. Birth after death. The magic of natality celebrated every first of February in Ireland. Brigid's day. "The Holy spirit is the rising sap ... coming from the sealed and guarded tomb" (Patrick Kavanagh).

Sometimes it is a matter of good hope as one crosses the *cap de bona Esperança* (Cape of Good Hope). Other times, false hope, when we wager on the wrong horse, bark up the wrong tree, are deceived or deceive ourselves. Other times again, it is hope against hope, as when Osip and Nadeshda Mandelstam's struggled against Stalin's executioners. Or, at best, it is another word for poetic imagination as one waits by doors and windows for everyday miracles to happen, for possibility to light the fuse of longing:

> I dwell in Possibility –
> A fairer House than Prose –
> More numerous of Windows –
> Superior – for Doors ...
>
> Of Visitors – the fairest –
> For Occupation – This –
> The Spreading wide my narrow Hands
> To gather Paradise –
> EMILY DICKENSON

Tá súil agam. Our deepest self-listening, waiting, keeping an eye out for the faint sound of hope and resilience, knowing that it alone can save our troubled world. The echo of a footfall approaching.

. . . .

Richard Kearney holds the Charles B. Seelig Chair of Philosophy at Boston College and has served as a Visiting Professor at University College Dublin, the University of Paris (Sorbonne), the Australian Catholic University and the University of Nice. He is the author of over twenty-five books on European philosophy and literature (including two novels and a volume of poetry) and has edited or co-edited twenty-one more. His most recent publications include Anatheism *(2012),* Reimagining the Sacred *(2015),* Carnal Hermeneutics *(2015) and* Twinsome Minds: An Act of Double Remembrance *(2018). He is currently international director of the Guestbook Project - Hosting the Stranger: Between Hostility and Hospitality. He currently lives in Boston, Massachusetts, where he is married to Anne Bernard and has two daughters, Simone and Sarah.*

"*Never deprive someone of hope; it might be all they have.*"

H. JACKSON BROWN, JR, AUTHOR

* * *

"*So now, Lord, what am I to hope for? My hope is in you.*"

PSALM 39:7

THE GIFT OF HOPE

. . . .

Patricia Scanlan

Without hope in our lives we would tread a long, dreary, hard path. Hope is a grace that is given to us. Even in the worst times of my life, when I was in chronic pain and beset by the difficulties it caused, I was lucky that I always hoped that there was light at the end of the tunnel. I've often found that at difficult times in my life that I'll hear something or read something, or someone will come into my life just when I need them. Years ago, when I was very down and waiting to have major surgery, a lovely card came to me out of the blue.

It said simply:

> *We believe in hope.*
> *"Hope does not disappoint."*
> (ROMANS 5:5)

What a lift it gave me. I felt it was a sign to look to the future with hope and to have faith that all would go well with my surgery. Today I can say gratefully that the operation I had made a huge difference. While I still have difficulties with my back, they are nothing compared to how bad it was then.

I kept that card and it is a reminder, especially in these very difficult days when we are facing such uncertainties, that it's important to keep hope in our lives. Simple things lift me. Nature is a wonderful balm to the spirit. I plant my seedlings and watch them grow into gorgeous flowers to nurture beautiful bees. I spend time with my nieces, nephews and great nephews. They are our future generation and they have *so* much to give. They inspire me.

In Shelley's immortal words.

"If winter comes, can spring be far behind?"

No matter how hard life is, if we can fan that little spark of hope that lies deep within us, it will sustain us and keep us going no matter what. If we have hope, we are rich. The best is yet to come.

. . . .

Patricia Scanlan was born in Dublin, where she still lives. She is a Number One bestselling author and has sold millions of books worldwide. Her novels, including the City Girl *trilogy, have sold over 1.4 million copies in Ireland alone. Her books are translated into many languages.*

*"People gain so much hope
when they know they are not
experiencing something alone."*

JOYCE RUPP, WRITER & RETREAT LEADER

* * *

*"May the God of hope fill you with
all joy and peace in your faith,
so that in the power of the Holy
Spirit you may be rich in hope."*

ROMANS 15:13

HOW TO HOLD HOPE LIGHTLY

Sharon Salzberg

When a new year dawns, we want to feel hopeful. Hope can encourage us to look forward confidently. The past few years have been tumultuous, and I've heard from many that they feel frightened or even foolish to hope that things in their world will be better. In other moments, we may find ourselves clinging to specific outcomes, believing "Life would be perfect if I could just get that thing, person, or experience".

We can learn to hold 'hope lightly'. That doesn't mean we're into hopelessness: in fact, it's quite the opposite. The opposite of hopelessness is considered to be love or connection. We move towards that connection with a sense of equanimity, the wisdom born of balance. Instead of trying to wrest control over life's changes, equanimity offers us space to see the world as it is without craving or fixation. It allows us the perspective that what's in front of us is not the end of the story. It's just what we can see right now.

We can ask ourselves, what brings hope? One way I've found healing through hope is remembering things in my life have been bleak before, and that I have responded well to adversity. I have also found hope in a sense of community and the experience of bearing the tough times together.

We feel the buoyancy of hope when we find ordinary things that can sustain our energy, give us optimism, and help us keep going. We can do our best, live according to our values, and acknowledge we may not always succeed at our aspirations. Yet the actions we're taking are honourable and those feelings of despair and inadequacy are part of the human condition. Through connection, we are reminded that we are a part of a broader context, and we are doing the best we can with what we have.

· ·

Sharon Salzberg is a meditation pioneer, world-renowned teacher and bestselling author. She is one of the first to bring mindfulness and loving kindness meditation to mainstream American culture over forty-five years ago, inspiring generations of meditation teachers and wellness influencers. Sharon is co-founder of The Insight Meditation Society in Barre, MA, and the author of twelve books, including the New York Times *bestseller,* Real Happiness, *now in its second edition, and her seminal work,* Lovingkindness. *Her forthcoming release,* Real Life: The Journey from Isolation to Openness and Freedom, *is set for release in April of 2023 from Flatiron Books. Her podcast,* The Metta Hour, *has amassed five million downloads and features interviews with thought leaders from the mindfulness movement and beyond.*

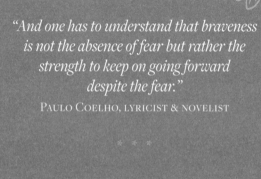

"And one has to understand that braveness is not the absence of fear but rather the strength to keep on going forward despite the fear."

PAULO COELHO, LYRICIST & NOVELIST

* * *

"Instruct those who are rich in this world's goods that they should not be proud and should set their hopes not on money, which is untrustworthy, but on God who gives us richly all that we need for our happiness."

1 TIMOTHY 6:17

WITNESSING THE PASSION AND LOVE OF

OTHERS

· · · · · · · · · ·

Stephen Donnelly

B y nature I'm an optimist. So I guess my first source of hope comes from within. But that'll only get you so far, particularly when you're the Minister for Health during a global pandemic.

I meet a lot of people through my job who are struggling in different ways. I meet patients who are looking for access to services and new treatments, and healthcare workers who are exhausted from the battle against Covid-19. I've also met families and communities reeling from the loss of loved ones taken by this terrible virus.

But that's also where I find hope; in other people. In the deep reservoir of compassion and love I am humbled by every day. Covid has tested our nation. And our nation's response has been one of solidarity and caring. Covid isn't as big a threat to most younger, healthy people. So why did so many take the vaccines? To keep other people safe. How did communities respond? By minding their neighbours who were more vulnerable; bringing them meals, checking in on them and meeting up for a chat over the garden wall.

Our healthcare workers mobilised like nothing we've ever seen. They kept going to work, even though that meant they were putting themselves at risk. They missed priceless time with their families, working longer hours to care for those who were sick. People from every walk of life came to work in our vaccine centres and testing centres. All over the country they spoke with me of the pride they had in being a part of something important. What were they so proud of? Helping to keep other people safe.

Every week I meet incredible people who are dedicating years of their lives to helping others: Community groups, patient groups, parents and, of course, our healthcare workers. Spending time with them, listening to their stories, witnessing their passion and their love – that's what makes me hopeful, even in these difficult times. How could it not.

. . . .

Stephen Donnelly is Minister for Health. He has been a TD since 2011. He is married with three children and lives in Co. Wicklow.

"Hope just means another world might be possible, not promised, not guaranteed. Hope calls for action; action is impossible without hope."

REBECCA SOLNIT, WRITER, HISTORIAN & ACTIVIST

* * *

"God, create in me a clean heart, renew within me a resolute spirit, do not thrust me away from your presence, do not take away from me your spirit of holiness. Give me back the joy of your salvation, sustain in me a generous spirit."

PSALMS 51:10-12

'HOPE IS TO ACT'

Teresa Buczkowska

We exist in a state of uncertainty, full of many movable elements that can turn our life one way or another. To alleviate the feeling of uncertainty we often resort to hope.

Hope is an expectation that the future we wish for will arrive despite any known and unknown obstacles. However, what is the basis for such expectation? As a person with a rather pragmatic approach to life, basing hope on an abstract expectation that is hung in a vacuum does not project confidence against uncertainty. Despite my pragmatism however I am a person full of hope, because without hope the uncertainty of life would be too frightening.

What is my hope rooted in? The word 'hope' in Polish translates as *'nadzieja'* and it derives from an old Slavic word that means 'to happen' but also 'to make' or 'to act'. Looking back, I understand now why inertia has been my biggest challenge to sustain hope. I can't say whether I started losing hope when I was falling into an inertia, or whether inertia entered my life when I started to lose hope. Either way 'hope/*nadzieja*' for me can only exist when the expectation for the future is supported by some forms of making that future.

I see hope when I see acts of resilience, even the smallest ones that are no more than just words of objections to injustice. I feel hope when I am standing up for the values and future I want to see for myself and for others. But most of all, experiencing and participating in collective acts of solidarity is the most nourishing source of hope. There is more power, motivation and energy when we act together towards the future we wish for than when we stand alone. It's easy to fall into an inertia when we are alone, and inertia is the biggest enemy of hope.

. . . .

Teresa Buczkowska is a migrant woman. She is a social anthropologist, migrant rights activist, and a writer. Teresa works as the Integration Manager at the Immigrant Council of Ireland. Teresa writes in English (which is her second language) and her main genre of writing is creative non-fiction. Teresa's main writing themes are: the notion of home, identity and belonging, grief and communal violence.

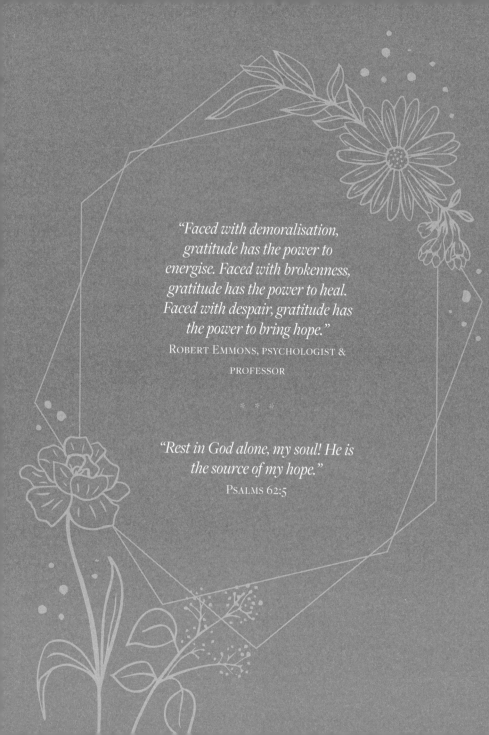

"Faced with demoralisation, gratitude has the power to energise. Faced with brokenness, gratitude has the power to heal. Faced with despair, gratitude has the power to bring hope."

ROBERT EMMONS, PSYCHOLOGIST & PROFESSOR

* * *

"Rest in God alone, my soul! He is the source of my hope."

PSALMS 62:5

HOPE IS NOT A DUTY

Terry Prone

The thing about hope is that pursuing it doesn't work, any more than pursuing happiness works.

You know them. You've seen them. The friends and relatives of someone who's just received a dire medical diagnosis. They go into overdrive, those friends and relatives. They bombard Dr Google. They browbeat hospital consultants. They insist, in the face of the bad news, on the primacy of hope, demanding clinical trials and new medicines. Sometimes, their insistence does the opposite of what is intended; it robs the central figure, the focus of the diagnosis, not just of hope, but of agency. They feel they have to 'keep fighting' and that they are somehow lesser if they're not hopeful. They become covert no-hopers, feeling obligated to express a hope in which they do not actually believe.

Hope isn't an obligation. Or a duty. It's an accidental by-product.

My wonderful husband, Tom Savage, spent three physically miserable years before he died, during which he never expressed hope, because he was too damn clever and realistic to bother trying to fool himself or anybody else. He just stayed true to his central belief, which was that life - and every relationship - should be a contest of generosities. Every day, in every encounter, he set out to improve other lives and make other people feel better about themselves. And every day, as a result, hope crept in behind him. Not an illogical, 'let's inspire' hope. A quiet sense that pain, age and physical limitations are no match for generosity, music, fun, loyalty and learning.

A kind of hope that is tranquil and private, and as sadly serene as the call of the mourning dove.

Terry Prone is Chairperson of The Communications Clinic, a leading author and a TV commentator on politics and current affairs.

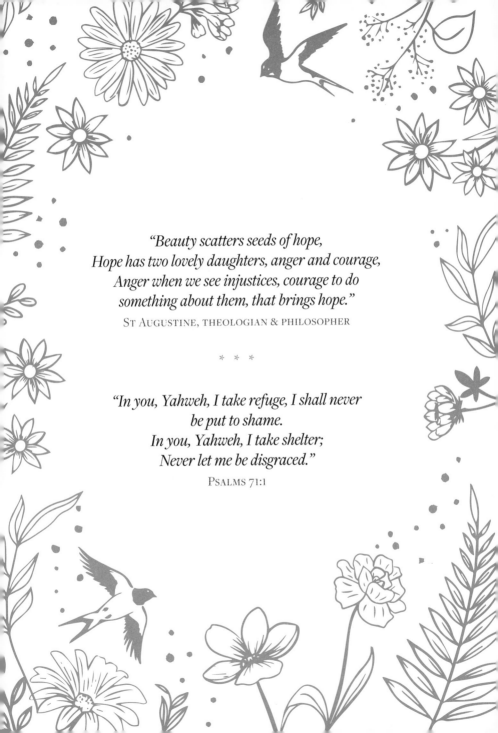

"Beauty scatters seeds of hope,
Hope has two lovely daughters, anger and courage,
Anger when we see injustices, courage to do
something about them, that brings hope."

St Augustine, theologian & philosopher

* * *

"In you, Yahweh, I take refuge, I shall never
be put to shame.
In you, Yahweh, I take shelter;
Never let me be disgraced."

Psalms 71:1

RENEWAL, REBIRTH AND REWARD

Tim Cullinan

Springtime provides the greatest hope for farming. It marks renewal and rebirth.

For farmers, it's the reward for their passion, experience and careful nurturing of their farm.

For some, it means newborn lambs and calves. It's the next generation of the herd or flock, signalling another successful cycle in the life of farming.

For others, they can see their crops begin to appear. It will take some time, but the successful establishment of the crop will bring a bountiful harvest later in the year.

Taking over from the previous generation and looking ahead to creating a better future is a special part of farming.

When I think back to when I started farming, I was filled with optimism about what I could do. It's a combination of learnings from the previous generation fused with ambition to take on new ideas.

The deep connection that farmers have to the land is what drives them to adapt and innovate.

Food is such a central part of our lives. Farmers understand the responsibility placed on them and the important role they have in society. Sometimes they feel undervalued, so their persistence is to be admired.

Despite all the challenges that farmers face, they have a resilience that gives me hope.

Keeping pace with dramatic changes in society and running a farm is not for the faint hearted.

But the agility of farmers to respond and chart a path for themselves is inspiring.

* *

Tim Cullinan was elected President of the Irish Farmers'
Association (IFA) in December 2019 by the 73,900
membership of the association. He is from Toomevara,
Co. Tipperary where he runs a pig enterprise, alongside
a feed mill operation in conjunction with the pig farm.
He is married to Margaret and has two sons, Brian and
Stephen. Tim has been heavily involved in the Irish Farmers'
Association over the past fifteen years, holding various
positions within the association.

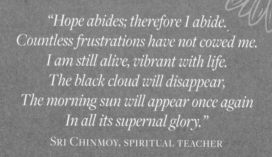

"Hope abides; therefore I abide.
Countless frustrations have not cowed me.
I am still alive, vibrant with life.
The black cloud will disappear,
The morning sun will appear once again
In all its supernal glory."

SRI CHINMOY, SPIRITUAL TEACHER

* * *

"For you alone are my hope, Lord,
Yahweh, I have trusted you since my youth,
I have relied on you since I was born,
You have been my portion from my
mother's womb,
And the constant theme of my praise."

PSALMS 71:5-6

'WHOEVER BROUGHT ME HERE WILL TAKE ME HOME'[1]

Michael Harding

W hat gives me hope is my desperate prayer, although I don't know if I'm doing anything right. After all I'm not following rules or adhering to the rituals of any church, mosque or temple.

I just wake up. And make it up. Because I couldn't get through a day without it. There's too much information falling on me, and my mind is inundated.

So, I try to keep the mind empty for that waking moment, and reach only for a mentor deity, be it Jesus, Buddha or the God of all things great and small. And I plead for help.

"Get me through this day."

After a few moments I begin to sense a stillness in the dawn light, in the quiet room, or even in the sound of distant cars and the hum of life outside, or the sigh of animals in the fields, or the wailing of sea birds.

They all command me to be still until I detect a presence beyond me, outside me, above me, below me, behind me and before me.

1   Rumi

And then I realise that I belong in this moment. I did not make myself. I realise that I was brought here to this day. And whoever brought me here will take me home.

I didn't fashion myself in the womb. I have been delivered here.

And my gateway to the fields of hope in this dystopian age of meaningless information, bombarding my senses at the turn of a thousand buttons, is to step into that field of silence first thing in the morning, and rest in it the moment I wake. Then hope flows like a river and courses through my veins like life itself, and the day begins to appear almost beautiful.

. . . .

Michael Harding is a short-story writer, novelist and playwright, born and raised in County Cavan. He lives in County Leitrim, near Arigna, and is a regular columnist with The Irish Times.

"Waking up this morning, I smile. Twenty-four brand new hours are before me. I vow to live fully in each moment and to look at all beings with eyes of compassion."

THICH NHAT HANH, MONK, AUTHOR & PEACE ACTIVIST

* * *

"Look, I am coming soon, and my reward is with me, to repay everyone as their deeds deserve."

REVELATION 22:12

LIFE WITHOUT HOPE IS VACUOUS

Patricia King

Throughout my career in the Trade Union movement, my daily motivation has been the *hope* that through our continuous representation and advocacy on behalf of workers in Ireland, we will ultimately achieve the improvements necessary to ensure that they all enjoy decent work with decent pay. This hope has helped define precisely the mission of our movement.

There are often days of despair and even despondency. On many occasions, particularly during the course of a difficult industrial dispute, I personally have had to dig deep to maintain a reasoned perspective. In such instances I usually take the time to probe the specific problem areas that need to be addressed, work hard to bring colleagues with me and *hope* that eventually reason will prevail.

As is the case in most peoples' lives, I have experienced some challenges and tests, sadness and happiness. Thankfully, as my life has progressed I have become more skilled at seeking out the reasons to be hopeful, even in circumstances when these are not immediately visible or evident. Once identified, I can then plot out the path to understanding or acceptance.

For me, the first verse of the late Emily Dickinson's poem, '*Hope is the Thing with Feathers*' conjures up very accurately how I feel about hope:

'Hope is the thing with feathers -
That perches in the soul -
And sings the tune without the words -
and never stops - at all -

While 'Hope' might be conceptual and intangible it gives us the impetus to carry on in the face of adversity.

· ·

Patricia King is the General Secretary of the Irish Congress
of Trade Unions (ICTU).

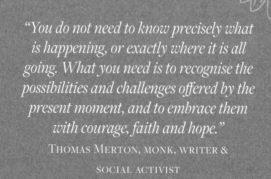

"You do not need to know precisely what is happening, or exactly where it is all going. What you need is to recognise the possibilities and challenges offered by the present moment, and to embrace them with courage, faith and hope."

THOMAS MERTON, MONK, WRITER & SOCIAL ACTIVIST

* * *

"Yahweh guards you from all harm Yahweh guards your life, Yahweh guards your comings and goings, henceforth and for ever."

PSALMS 121:7-8

STICK A FEATHER IN THE GROUND AND

IT MIGHT GROW A CHICKEN

· ·

Rosaleen Linehan

You are an actor. My advice is if you are lucky enough to get a part in a film, there are two things you must not pretend to be competent in: horse riding and ice skating.

So why did I say to Sr Stan that I could write this?

Well here goes: Hope for everyone. Hope is a part of a balanced daily life. For actors it is more. It helps us through the thorny path of rejections and allows us to come out ready for more at the other end.

Fergus (my late husband) and myself wrote a mini-musical based on *The Char Woman's Daughters* by James Stephens. We called it *Mary Makebelieve*. Mrs Makebelieve and her beautiful young daughter lived in unspeakable poverty in a Dublin tenement in the early Twentieth Century. Mother was always hoping that a letter would arrive from her uncle Patrick in America with news of riches beyond belief.

At one point Mary loses patience with her dreaming and chides her "this is never going to happen Ma, we'll die like this". Mother fights back. Fergus simply used Stephens' words for the song:

Around every corner
The whole world is waitin
It's gladness, it's sadness
It's peace and it's strife,
From a church or a taverrn
A saint, or a sinner
May step on the pavement
And change your whole life.

Mrs Makebelieve's dreams, of course, do come true. It is a fantasy, and happiness abounds.

In this fractured threatened world we are living in I am clinging on to ... not the letter from America, but some slow but sure change to build a possible future for my grandchildren. And the future generations. Indeed I have a fervent hope that it is they who will bring it about.

Yes, I have faith and hope in them.

. . . .

Rosaleen Linehan has probably been acting since she was born,
but officially for about sixty five years. She is best known for
acting the clown with Des Keogh in some memorable revues,
mainly written by her husband Fergus. Then some serious
stuff: Brian Friel, Sean O Casey, Shakespeare, though even
they had a great comic element, and back with Des in Beckett's
Endgame. *She has four children and nine grandchildren.*

"Isn't it the moment of most profound doubt that gives birth to new certainties? Perhaps hopelessness is the very soil that nourishes human hope; perhaps one could never find sense in life without first experiencing its absurdity."

VACLAV HAVEL, WRITER

* * *

"He alone is my rock, my safety, my stronghold, so that I stand unwavering."

PSALMS 62:6

JANUARY JOYS

· · · · · · · · · · · · · · · · · ·

Linda Doyle

For the last several years, I have been a judge in the BT Young Scientist & Technology Exhibition (BTYSTE). Judging takes place across three days in the dark month of January in the RDS, Dublin. I usually arrive with a mild sense of panic knowing there is a pile of work building up back in my office but, within minutes of arriving, these feelings disappear because - as anyone who has ever been to the BTYSTE will know - when you enter the exhibition hall, you become submerged in a world full of hope. I often say that going to the BTYSTE in January gives me enough hope for the rest of the year.

At times, it can be very hard to feel hopeful: our planet is under threat, democracy across the globe has been eroded, and we are still not in a fully post-pandemic world. The BTYSTE gives me great hope, not because I think science and technology is the full answer to any of these challenges, but because of the ambition and creativity of the young students who participate.

Being a judge means spending time with different individuals and teams and hearing their stories about their work. Every year there are projects tackling climate action and biodiversity loss, projects about disability and inclusivity, projects about making the world a better place in all sorts of ways. Every year you see young people who fully grasp the need to support what they say with evidence, and who are not afraid of learning new things. And, every year, there are students who reach far beyond the school curriculum in ways that astound.

And when the BTYSTE is over, I am fortunate enough to return to Trinity College where I am surrounded by more fantastic people who are also boldly questioning the world around them, by striving to understand the past as well as imagining and building different more hopeful futures.

Surrounded by people like this, it is so much easier to feel hopeful.

• •

A native of Togher in Cork city, Linda Doyle is the Provost and President of Trinity College Dublin. Previously, she was Professor of Engineering and the Arts, and also served as Trinity's Dean of Research. She was the founding director of CONNECT - Ireland's national research centre for telecommunications networks, which included several hundred researchers across ten Irish higher education institutions.

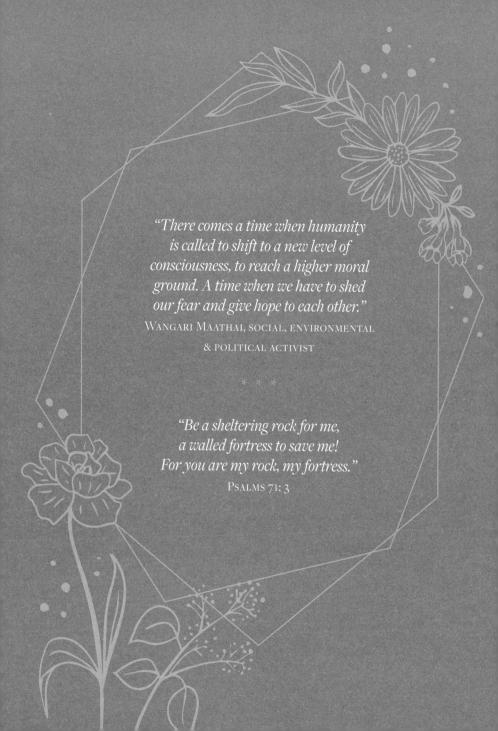

"There comes a time when humanity
is called to shift to a new level of
consciousness, to reach a higher moral
ground. A time when we have to shed
our fear and give hope to each other."
WANGARI MAATHAI, SOCIAL, ENVIRONMENTAL
& POLITICAL ACTIVIST

* * *

"Be a sheltering rock for me,
a walled fortress to save me!
For you are my rock, my fortress."
PSALMS 71: 3

GRASPING FOR MERCURY

Orla Guerin

A t times I don't hope. At times I can't. It slips from my grasp, like mercury, these days more than ever.

As I write death is raining from the skies in Ukraine. Civilians are hiding in basements, seeking sanctuary from Russian shells and missiles. Tanks have been unleashed on apartment blocks. Families, homes and communities have been destroyed. In our time there is war in Europe on a scale not seen since 1945. What I have seen on the ground since Russia invaded its neighbour – a sovereign democratic state - makes it hard to write, or think, or speak of hope. The concept seems misplaced amid a new landscape of scorched earth and mass graves. But what I have witnessed on Ukrainian soil is resilience, strength and courage.

For those forced to flee their homeland – more than five million in the first few months of the war – there has been shelter and support in neighbouring states. Ireland too opened its doors, in the face of an existing housing crisis. People running for their lives were given a place to go. Children were enrolled at school. That perhaps is hope made real – the capacity to respond to the suffering of others, to look at them and see a reflection of ourselves. And critical in all of that is the decision not to simply turn away.

Having covered conflicts in many countries, for many years, I also draw hope from the example of Northern Ireland. What seemed impossible throughout my childhood and teens in Dublin came to pass. The Troubles were brought to an end. The guns fell silent. And that silence echoed around the world, lending a measure of hope to those mired in conflicts elsewhere.

The peace may be imperfect. Divisions and deep scars remain. But few would return to the bombs and the bullets. In this, there is hope.

· ·

Dublin-born journalist Orla Guerin is the BBC's International Correspondent, based in Istanbul. In her long career this veteran foreign correspondent has held a succession of high-profile postings. Her work has been recognised with awards in Ireland, the UK, the USA, France and Italy. Since joining the BBC in 1995 she has been based in Cairo, Islamabad, Johannesburg, Jerusalem and Rome, as well as spending periods on attachment in Los Angeles and Moscow. Prior to joining the BBC, she was Eastern Europe Correspondent for RTÉ. She took up that role in 1990 - at the age of 23 - and has been in motion ever since.

"The care of the Earth is our most ancient and most worthy, and after all, our most pleasing responsibility. To cherish what remains of it and to foster its renewal is our only hope."

WENDELL BERRY, WRITER & ENVIRONMENTAL ACTIVIST

* * *

"Can a woman forget her baby at the breast, feel no pity for the child she has borne? Even if these were to forget, I shall not forget you."

ISAIAH 49:15

HOPE IN THE TIME OF A PANDEMIC

Mike Ryan

These last few years with Covid-19 have challenged us as individuals, as families, as communities and as societies. Many of us have been pushed to the limit: personally, professionally, physically and mentally.

As individuals we were often separated from friends and families. As families we were often scattered and isolated. As a society, we were confronted with uncertainty and fear that led in many cases to amazing acts of connection and solidarity, but also to misinformation, exclusion and stigma.

After endless months of renewed pandemic waves, new variants, new sacrifices, we all reached a point of physical, mental and spiritual exhaustion.

At WHO, I have seen our wonderful staff and partners pushing their limits every day, every evening, every weekend to deliver life-saving information, guidance, technical support and supplies to countries and communities, while still striving to understand this virus better and develop more effective interventions.

We all ran a marathon at the speed of a sprint. Many of us were far away from our homes and families, many of us were under personal attack.

And still, none of us ever considered giving up. We were driven by hope.

The hope that is brought by solidarity with others, by sacrifice for others.

The hope for a better and safer tomorrow.

It gave us hope to see the enormous public support for our courageous healthcare workers who risked their own health and lives to deliver care to others, while often separated from their own families. They were the last human touch and contact for many dying people.

It gave us hope to see the resilience of our communities, their willingness to put up with uncertainty and fear as well as their inspiring acts of kindness and solidarity

It gave us hope to see the unprecedented innovation of scientists across the world, who feverishly worked together to develop better information, vaccines, therapeutics and diagnostics.

It gave us hope, when we saw our connectedness leveraged as our strength, not our weakness; when that connectedness generated solidarity, not fear and stigma; listening not shouting; good information not disinformation; cooperation not competition; sharing not hoarding.

What gives me hope is that we have a new generation of young people connected to sustainability, solidarity and fairness. A generation that will work to care for our injured planet and ecosystem, and that understands that we cannot leave anyone behind on our collective journey into the future.

It is our responsibility not to forget the hard lessons learned during Covid-19 and to turn this brutal experience into a precious opportunity.

We have learned how to prepare better for the next pandemic. How to prepare ourselves, our communities, our countries and our planet. I hope we will do just that.

. . . .

Originally from Sligo, Dr Michael Ryan is Executive Director of the World Health Organisation's (WHO) Health Emergencies Programme. He has been at the forefront of managing acute risks to global health since he first joined WHO in 1996, with the newly established unit to respond to emerging and epidemic disease threats. He has worked in conflict affected countries and led many responses to high impact epidemics. He is a founding member of the Global Outbreak Alert and Response Network (GOARN), which has aided the response to hundreds of disease outbreaks around the world.

"If we were really looking at this world, we would be moved a hundred times a day, by the flowers at the side of the road, the people we meet, by all that brings us messages of our goodness and the goodness of all things."

ANDREW HARVEY, POET & PHILOSOPHER

* * *

"I lift up my eyes to the mountains; where is my help to come from? My help comes from Yahweh who made heaven and earth."

PSALMS 121:1-2

LAUGHTER HELPS!

. . . .

Phil Ní Sheaghdha

When you think about having hope or feeling hopeful it is difficult to conceptualise how central this emotion is to the ability to face the trials and tribulations of life. In all my interactions with patients, it is the simplest yet most important motivator to keep going. The ability to laugh and to find the funny side of life helps enormously with the ability to hope.

Laughter is something magical; sometimes you hear it and it lifts a bleakness you did not know you had. Some people laugh silently but their body moves, their faces become entirely alive and you can almost see into their soul. Some people laugh like their life depends on the next breath, I especially love the feeling of uncontrollable laughter, when I think of the people I love to meet and enjoy spending time with, they all have the same thing in common, they enjoy a good laugh.

I recently met a group of student nurses, who had worked during the pandemic on Covid wards, some of them were scared and many of the patients they looked after died. They started talking about the experience and then one of them said "remember the morning I couldn't get the door open?" They all burst into laughter. They added to and embellished the story, and they all laughed.

Solidarity sometimes is the sound of a group seeing the funny side of life and seeing it together, even when faced with a terrible crisis.

I want to tell you about Jack, he was an American, born in an area where Irish immigrants lived. He became friends with a group of Irish neighbours, and said they made him laugh and enjoy life. At age eighty-eight he got diagnosed with a terminal condition. He was facing a short, bleak future. He rang one of his old pals, long since returned to Ireland, and told him. His friend encouraged him to make a last trip to Ireland. One morning before he left, he was shaving and said he heard a strange sound he barely recognised, it was his own laughter. He made the trip, had great laughs and he felt it was better than fine wine!

That feeling of spontaneous laughter can often be the best medicine of all.

. . . .

Phil Ní Sheaghdha, from the west Kerry Gaeltacht – trained as a nurse in Dublin and worked in many countries in ICU nursing before returning to Ireland and becoming involved with the trade union INMO. She has worked with the union since 1998 and was appointed General Secretary in 2018. A passionate belief in fairness and social solidarity keeps the focus.

*"Hope is the dream of a
waking man."*

ARISTOTLE, PHILOSOPHER &
POLYMATH

* * *

*"For my hope is in you
all day long - such is your
generosity, Yahweh."*

PSALMS 25:5

WHERE THERE IS LIFE THERE IS HOPE:

WHERE THERE IS HOPE THERE IS LIFE

Sr Regina McHugh

The much quoted letter to Corinthians 13, ends with the words "three things remain: faith, hope and love, and the greatest of these is love". Yet without faith and hope to make the 'three legged stool' solid, we can see how love can become wobbly; that it never stands up.

We speak a great deal about faith and love, but somehow there can be little enough space in between for *hope* – it seems like the proverbial 'middle child', sandwiched in between affirmation about the priority of faith and the excellence of love.

We often say "where there is life, there is hope". We can turn it around and say "where there is hope, there is life". Hope is the very heart and centre of the human being. There is simply nothing more central to human life. Hope keeps us alive. Hope inspires us to press ahead despite the difficulties. Hope brings a willingness to cultivate within ourselves whatever kindles light, and to shine that light into the darkest places. Hope is the conviction that you survived all you survived, so that you can be a good role-model, a person who focuses, not on what was lost, but on what is still here and on the work you are called to do. Hope challenges us to live life and to live it in the fullest possible way.

We simply cannot live without hope. But hope does not start with us. It starts with God. Our calling to our Poor Clare way of life, takes on a new meaning since it is 'rooted' in daily prayer. For prayer, 'believing prayer', is based on the certainty that God is working for us, with us and in us. He is the one who has promised to love us, never leave us, be strong when we are weak, provides direction when we are lost and wisdom whenever we ask for it. With God all things are possible. We trust in his plans for our future, for "yesterday has gone, tomorrow has not yet come and we have only today to make him known, loved and served". We are grateful for the many opportunities given us to bring hope into people's lives by our prayerful support and our compassion for them. Many people either directly by phone, or indirectly through others, by email and by letter, ask us to pray for them and we are privileged to do so. The hope that we offer is prayerful, and our prayer is hopeful, as there is a hope dimension to their request.

Mother Teresa of Calcutta, in her lifetime, wanted to create hope for every single person … "We must give *hope* always *hope*," she said. Her conviction was that by bringing hope into a multitude of lives by concern for the individual sufferer, we could help our troubled world on the brink of despair. *Where there is life there is hope.*

. . . .

Sr Regina McHugh is a native of Co. Westmeath. She trained as a nurse and is happily living, for the past thirty-eight years, with the Poor Clare Community in Ennis, Co. Clare.

"It is a huge danger to pretend that awful things do not happen. But you need enough hope to keep going. I am trying to make hope. Flowers grow out of darkness."

CORITA KENT, ARTIST & EDUCATOR

* * *

"Yahweh takes care of all their bones, not one of them will be broken."

PSALMS 34:20

CROCUS

Brother Richard Hendrick

Once, long ago,
during a winter more grey within
than cold without,
when the house was filled
with seeming endless
sadness, and anger
and emptiness,
I came down one morning
to a chilled and silent kitchen
to discover that outside,
a crocus had bloomed overnight,
under the old cherry tree,
in a place none had ever bloomed before.

How had it come there on that day,
in that place?
Bird-carried, wind-blown,
or old planting stirred anew?
But, why wonder at its coming?
All it asked of me
was to be seen.

I stood, still,
empty kettle in hand,
staring into the grey garden,
now sunlit, with the yellow frail petals
of an unexpected
and unlooked-for flower.
It lasted just long enough
for us to hear,
behind the song of sorrow
we were singing in that house then,
a note of hope, a sound of spring,
not now, but coming.

I knew then, and for evermore,
that at the right time, and in the right place,
looked at in the right way,
even a tiny yellow crocus
can be a word from the Word.

So today I know that
when sadness sings her song
around my roots,
it is okay,
it is beautiful,
it is necessary,
but also it is an invitation
to wait and watch
for the yellow crocus
to bloom again,
as it always will,
announcing angel-like
the nearness of spirit's spring,
not now, perhaps,
but always coming.[1]

---

1   Br Richard Hendrick, *Still Points: A Guide to Living the Mindful Meditative Way*, Dublin: Hachette Ireland, 2022.

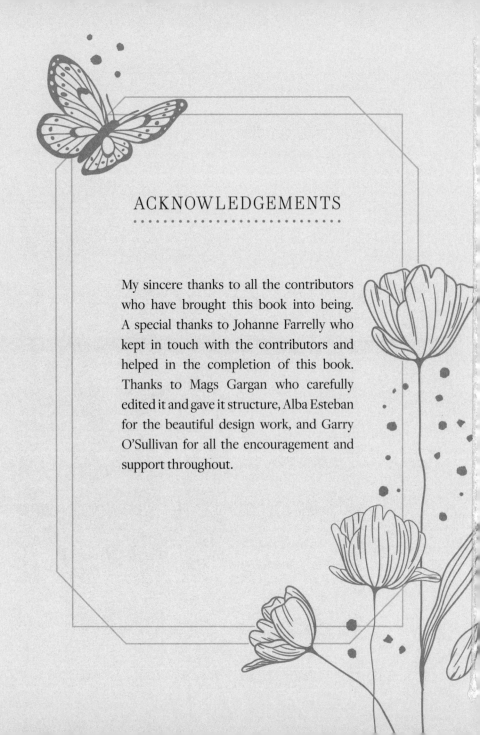

ACKNOWLEDGEMENTS

My sincere thanks to all the contributors who have brought this book into being. A special thanks to Johanne Farrelly who kept in touch with the contributors and helped in the completion of this book. Thanks to Mags Gargan who carefully edited it and gave it structure, Alba Esteban for the beautiful design work, and Garry O'Sullivan for all the encouragement and support throughout.